MW00452537

WALKING A CROOKED SMILE

AN INNER JOURNEY TO PEACE

JERRY WONG

Published by Peaceful Warrior Arts Inc.
in partnership with Influence Publishing Inc., June 2022
ISBN: 978-1-7781547-0-6

Copyright © 2022 Jerry Wong
All rights reserved. No part of this publication may be reproduced, stored in or introduced into a retrieval system, or transmitted, in any form, or by any means (electronic, mechanical, photocopying, recording or otherwise) without the prior written permission of the publisher. This book is sold subject to the condition that it shall not, by way of trade or otherwise, be lent, resold, hired out, or otherwise circulated without the publisher's prior consent in any form of binding or cover other than that in which it is published and without a similar condition including this condition being imposed on the subsequent purchaser.

Editing: Danielle Anderson
Proofreading: Lee Robinson
Typesetting and Cover Design: Tara Eymundson and Jerry Wong
Cover Art: Jerry Wong/Judy Wong/Bailey Wong

DISCLAIMER: Readers of this publication agree that neither Jerry Wong, nor his publisher will be held responsible or liable for damages that may be alleged as resulting directly or indirectly from the use of this publication. Neither the publisher nor the author can be held accountable for the information provided by, or actions resulting from, accessing these resources.

While all the stories in this book are true, some names and identifying details have been changed to protect the privacy of the people involved.

DEDICATION

For my family—the young ones as well as the elders—and in memory of my niece Bailey, our family angel.

For all Peaceful Warriors.

For a peaceful, balanced future for *all* beings.

Bailey

Still – the smile so pure and gentle
Memory rolls down my cheeks
Stirring to depths not shown
I'm again between worlds!
It's where we meet.

TESTIMONIALS

"Since 1972, Sensei Jerry Wong has been a close friend. He was already experienced in classical martial arts Kung Fu when we met, and he was very passionate about understanding the Karate side. We practised Shorei-Kan Karate-Do together, and now he has reached the fifth Dan Black Belt Shihan Degree. He is also skilled in Chi Kung and is a wonderful graphic artist who continues to create art to this day. To me, I think of his art like Karate. He has a deep spiritual connection to animals and their well-being, and he seeks peace and healing for nature.

"Chinese Classic Kung Fu (Shaolin Zen) came to Okinawa and evolved to Karate, so they are derived from the same ancestor. Sensei Jerry Wong absorbed the maternal Karateology education. He is a very warm-hearted, compassionate person and is a great example of the combination of knowledge and self-defence. He carries these two-way martial arts—he has Bunbu Nido Spirit (heart/martial arts) secrets inside his body. In Okinawa, we call these extremely talented people Bushi and Shihan. That is him."

Tomoaki Koyabu
Student of Seikichi Toguchi Sensei of Shorei-Kan Karate-Do

"It is rare to have someone with the special talents that Jerry possesses come into our lives. I was the owner of Beau, who you will read about in this book. Jerry Wong was referred to us when we were desperate to help Beau out from a terminal diagnosis. What was a two-week prognosis became a two-year journey of Beau enjoying life again. Seeing my other rescue dogs respond to Jerry throughout the years has been even more enlightening. I am so grateful for Jerry Wong and am thrilled that he has chosen to put his special work forth in this book for others to experience through his stories."

Bev Benwick, MAL

"Compelling to the end, Sensei Jerry Wong delves into diverse and deeply spiritual experiences he's had with humans and a variety of animals. These are unforgettable stories rooted in martial arts teachings and animal communication, with peace and harmony for ALL beings as the unifying theme. This is a book that will have pride of place on my bookshelf, with a space left for a sequel to stand beside it!

"Sensei Jerry's lifelong commitment to the seeking of the truth is clear, and this gem of a book is the vehicle that will allow his message that we are all ONE to now spread abroad. Please let there be a sequel!"

Heather Rankin, SAMP, SAAP
Flowing River Pet Therapy, former student of Sensei Jerry

"Reading Jerry Wong's book is like being taken on a guided journey into the mystical world of a Peaceful Warrior. The insights he attributes to his life experiences have created a truly inspiring narrative.

"Thank you, Jerry, for your courage, wisdom, and perseverance. I know your book will help me with my journey—and who knows, maybe one day we will be standing on that mountain top, enjoying the view together."

Bill Basaraba

CONTENTS

DEDICATION iii

TESTIMONIALS v

FOREWORD ix

INTRODUCTION xi

PART 1: WE ARE ALL ONE

1   Song 3

2   Re-member 11

3   Energy/Chi 19

4   Human Truth 23

PART 2: MARTIAL ARTS FOR PEACE

5   A Lifetime of Lessons 35

6   Lessons from My Mentors 41

7   DY and His Do 45

8   What the Martial Arts Teach Us 47

9   The Mountain 53

10   Lessons from the Mountain 63

11   Martial Arts for the Disabled 67

PART 3: ENERGY HEALING AND ENERGY FLOW

12   Energy Healing 73

13   Examples of Energy Healing 77

14   Where Attention Goes, Energy Flows 85

PART 4: ANIMAL COMMUNICATION

15   Wings to Fly 93

16   Kokoro 99

17   Scout and Rex 105

18   The Intuition of Horses 111

19   Tawny and Mamie 117

20   Unconditional Love 121

21   Animals as Natural Healers 127

22   Bring Heaven to Earth 131

23   KT and KIT 137

24   Mini Lessons 147

PART 5: THE OTHER SIDE OF THE VEIL

25   Life – Stranger than Fiction 155

26   Dave Wong 163

27   Message in a Dream 167

28   Contact While in a Coma 171

29   Warning from the Other Side 175

CONCLUSION 181

ABOUT THE AUTHOR 189

FOREWORD

By Beth Harris, Peaceful Warrior in training

Welcome to this gem of a book! It is a heartfelt offering of intimate life experiences from Sensei Jerry Wong, and it fills me with faith, hope, and wonder. I so appreciate his ability to humbly surrender his ego to a loving presence larger than himself, grounding himself to and interacting with life beyond the five senses—*especially* through animals.

I'm a preacher's kid, and prior to meeting Sensei in my fifties, I had become someone who sought a more mystical relationship with the Holy Spirit, trying to live life in service to Love. I also secretly dreamt of being able to heal people. The day I met Sensei, Spirit turned my head to notice him walking by and to take note. We met about thirty minutes later at a school playground. He was instructing his grandsons on how to do a martial arts pose on the slide, and I smiled. I knew he was going to be an interesting man. We started a conversation and connected through our mutual service to Love and experiences with Spirit, although he was at a whole different level than I was. He took me on as his student and began to teach me Qigong.

After a short time of study, however, Spirit abruptly hit the pause button on my training with Sensei. Injuries I sustained during a hit-and-run accident marked the beginning of a five-year period of recovery, upheaval, and heartbreaking loss. The Qigong breathing I had learned helped ground me during this shift, and I never stopped doing what minimal exercises I could do, even if they were only mental or visual. All the lessons he taught me helped to keep me afloat through this turbulent time.

These lessons also helped when I was having a difficult time with my ever-growing, severely disabled teenage son. If I was feeling overwhelmed, I would do some Qigong breathing and visualizations to help ground myself, clear my mind, and open my heart so I could try to "hear" what my boy needed.

While the dust of these events began to settle, Sensei told me about his book and asked me to read his first draft. It was EXACTLY what I needed, and I was inspired by his courage to share his heart in such a way. This book affirms my own spiritual experiences, which I have previously brushed off and doubted, and offers me the hope of connecting more deeply with my non-verbal autistic son.

The lessons in this book also became a mirror by which I recognize my own spiritual autism. Just like autistic people are unable to fully process the world that most of us experience with our five senses, so am I unable to fully process the world beyond them. I know that my son, like Sensei, is in communication with that world beyond, so I see myself as "spiritually autistic," unable to cognitively function within that larger scope of life. I have now been inspired to stop doubting myself and have faith that I can one day be able to communicate in a functional way with my son.

Sensei lays his heart bare in this book, and his messages can be easily understood if you are open to receiving them. After you have read it fully, continue to pick it up when fear seeks to close your heart, drawing you into its room of despair. On any given day, you might read something that will be just what you need in that moment and be once again immersed in the peace and calm that is the natural flow of life as a Peaceful Warrior.

Thank you, Sensei, for this gift! Thank you for being able to navigate two worlds as one, and for your commitment to serve. I am forever grateful for your teachings, and *Walking a Crooked Smile* is already one of my life's treasured companions.

INTRODUCTION

This project began years ago as a letter to my first grandson. It was intended to be a private, heartfelt communication which would include thoughts and words to support him as he progressed along his spiritual journey.

Well, I did get the letter started, but then things happened (or didn't happen) and I never finished it. At this point, I've procrastinated long enough that a second grandson and a few more new additions have been born into our family, so writing a single letter no longer seems appropriate.

Back when I was composing the letter, though, I showed my draft to some of my senior martial arts students for their opinions. After reading it, they suggested I use this letter as a foundation for a book, as they thought the teachings should be shared with the public. After giving it a lot of thought, I realized that if my writings could benefit even one person on their spiritual journey, then this would be a worthy endeavour.

I have to admit that working on this book has been a bit of a struggle, as I do not find writing to be one of my natural talents. However, I have a feeling that the snail's pace of advancement was intended to be a life lesson for me. It has given me time to reappraise my thoughts and actions, to mature further spiritually, and to hone my skills as a Warrior for Peace.

My rationale for the title of this book is tied into the overall message. It is based on my personal belief that every human on Earth is destined to "walk a crooked mile" (or path) as we journey through life. If you look back on your steps in life as though you are looking at a map, you won't find a straight line running from infancy to where you stand now. Instead, you'll find a series of crooked lines meandering from one major life event to another.

You and I are meant to learn experientially. There are certain situations we experience in our daily lives that we may not necessarily want, but that we *need* for our spiritual growth. We all fall down, make mistakes, and lose our way. And while each of us has the right to choose whether or not we consciously strive to learn through our experiences, many are unaware that we have this choice at all. As a result, we feel victimized and powerless.

I believe we have come to this earthly plane to learn our natural WAY TO BE—to learn to allow our (higher) self to express peace, harmony, nonviolence, and love. We humans can't control every facet of our lives, nor can we control the lives of others. But once we realize that the lives we have been given are a gift, we can live each moment with a positive, grateful attitude and follow our own inner guidance system (once we discover that we have one).

Gratitude is the secret key. Whenever you are in a state of gratitude, it becomes easier to drop into your heart and consciously connect with Source (also named God, Nature, Spirit, whatever you may call it). Whenever you are connected to Source, you're in Truth. To be in Truth is to be in trust, and to enjoy Heaven on Earth. Learn to be in this state as often as possible, and you will achieve inner harmony.

So, the title of this book refers to a feeling, not a thought. It's about living your life from your heart, not your head. It's about learning through our life experiences while being connected to Source, about being empowered, and about living from a place of peace.

Scattered randomly throughout this book are writings and drawings which I hope will help convey what my words cannot adequately express. I created these while practising processes known as automatic writing and automatic drawing. These processes happen when the spirit world wishes to communicate with us through written or illustrated messages. During these times, I place myself in a calm, meditative state and call upon my spirit guides and other loving entities to channel their messages through me. Some messages seem fairly straightforward while others are quite cryptic and require considerable pondering.

These writings and images are not produced from my own concepts or thoughts. Yes, my hand physically does the writing or drawing, but I am setting my conscious mind aside, allowing myself to become a facilitator—a vehicle through which the spirit guides and other entities can communicate.

I have chosen one particular automatic drawing to place on the front cover. For this drawing, the spirit of my deceased sister Judy came through. She guided my hands, gently placing my head on the paper and having me trace the profile of my face with my pen, then lifting my head off the paper and adding a smile. She then drew an arrow pointing to my smile. Could she be simply advising me to "walk my crooked smile"?

Judy signed her name at the bottom right area, and it appears that my deceased niece Bailey printed her name across my forehead.

Just as quickly

All will be-come

Peace

An example of automatic writing.

My involvement in the areas of art and design, Chi Kung (the study of our life force energy), Chinese and Okinawan martial arts, intuitive energy healing, acupressure, and telepathic animal communication have influenced me profoundly. I am grateful for my experiences and have benefited from them in many ways. Over the years, my training in these areas evolved into a natural blending or synthesis of ancient and modern methods, serving as a map to guide me on my life path. In this book, I share with you some of my personal stories; perhaps you will be able to relate to some of them. Hopefully, these stories will raise questions in your mind that will help you progress along your own spiritual journey. I've chronicled these memories and experiences from my life as factually as possible, but for privacy reasons I've changed most of the names.

At this point I would like to make it known that everything written here is from my own beliefs and conclusions to date. Years ago, I received some wise advice from Kaicho Seikichi Toguchi, my Karate master. Kaicho (a title given to the principal of a school) suggested that I teach or share mainly from lessons I have learned through direct life experiences, and not to rely too heavily on the words of others to find my Truths. So, these are my understandings, based mainly on my own personal experiences. My hope is that this information will serve you as well, even if in some small way, on your own individual journey toward peace and well-being.

Part 1

WE ARE ALL ONE

Automatic drawing by author.

1

SONG

One summer evening in 1965, my friend DY and I were walking through Vancouver's "Skid Row" on our way to play a game of pool at a local billiard hall. Heading toward us from the opposite direction was a visibly drunk, bedraggled-looking couple in the heat of a huge fight. The man was being beaten mercilessly by his female companion, who kept slamming him over his head and shoulders with her handbag and kicking at his legs. He was bent over in pain, trying unsuccessfully to shield himself and walk at the same time; she was in a frenzy, yelling and swearing in rage. And as we quickly sidestepped out of their battle zone to avoid getting hit, I could hear a song coming from a transistor radio in the man's jacket pocket.

It was Jackie DeShannon's song, "What the World Needs Now Is Love."

"What the world needs now is love, sweet love.
It's the only thing that there's just too little of...."

DY and I stood there with grins on our faces, watching the couple stagger and scuffle up the street while this song called out for love. It was both funny and sad at the same time.

For some reason, this little scenario jumped out at me and remains etched in my mind to this day. It was as if this couple was intentionally putting on a skit as a life lesson for us. Their outburst seemed like a microcosmic display of the way our world has become. A song is being whispered constantly by our higher selves, calling out for love and peace, but the song is falling on deaf ears.

Automatic drawing by author.

The Current State of Our World

Opening up is surely the

Way for peace ---

Universe calls

listen to angels near ---

they want to sing and

say much to you so let

your energy flow as paper

for their writing of wishes

to be determining future of

history in all ---

I believe that many of us on this planet are now aware, on some deep level, that we are in the midst of change. This change is not so much taking place in a physical sense (externally), but rather as a shifting of consciousness (internally).

We humans are passing through a transitional period which I believe will lead us from our current state of fear and illusion to one of love and the seeking of truth. Stirring deep within ourselves is the realization, either conscious or unconscious, that our negative feelings of despair and isolation are rooted in the (false) belief that we are separate from each other, separate from all other species, and separate from Source.

Humanity is now in the process of awakening to the truth that we are all connected, interdependent, and whole. We are not ALONE; we are ALL ONE.

As we open to this new paradigm of oneness, we will begin to see with new eyes and hear with new ears. Hope will replace despair, and we will become aware of our unique potential to transform the world around us and to co-create *peace and harmony for ALL beings.*

We all yearn for Heaven on Earth—a world filled with peace, harmony, love, and joy for all beings—but there is much work to be done to bring about this reality. We must first make a conscious choice to walk the path toward peace with purpose and courage; only then can we work together as Peaceful Warriors and become catalysts for elevating the consciousness of our world.

We humans are climbing the mountain of life together. Spiritually, we are each at various levels on this mountain—some are at the base, a few are nearing the peak, and most are scattered at various levels in between. I can only view and speak from my own spot on the mountain, and hopefully what I'm sharing will resonate with you and assist you in finding your own way.

People around the globe have the same simple needs, regardless of differences in race, religion, political beliefs, or any other "dividing" factor. We all want a good quality of life, access to food and shelter, a safe place to raise our families, and the opportunity to enjoy our lives in peace and harmony. With this in mind, don't you think that meeting these needs can be accomplished by working together as one?

Unfortunately, the human spirit has been broken somewhere along the line. We've been taught the false belief that we are all separate from one another, and this has created loneliness and hopelessness in this world. Struggling in a state of fear and chaos, we've been ignoring the song! We feel overwhelmed and powerless to affect change, and we have adopted a herd mentality in order to survive.

Open your eyes – Look beyond

I'm convinced that ordinary people, both individually and collectively, CAN rise above our current state of dysfunction and chaos to transform our reality. I believe that we humans are stirring from our slumber. We are now awakening, and a shift in our collective consciousness is taking root.

Just like the little scenario back in 1965, which hinted at the human condition to me, many recent global events have revealed much that was hidden from the masses for so long. It appears there is a quickening of events in many established fields: economics, politics, global health, and more. We are beginning to distinguish falseness from truth. We are becoming aware of our true powers and the responsibility that comes with them. You, along with every human being that exists on Mother Earth, are now beginning to hear the whispers of the song calling for love!

As we embrace the simple fact that we are all one, we can unlock our unlimited potential and find the power within ourselves to make changes to this world.

Automatic drawing by author.

Love or Fear?

Take control of destiny
to always watch
energy pulse forward
not energy backwards

Each and every one of us has the power of choice in how we think, what we say, and the actions (or inactions) we take. We walk with dignity and strength when we focus with positive awareness and believe in ourselves. Together we can accomplish whatever it takes to bring Heaven to Earth, but we need to decide whether or not to try.

We humans are thinkers—thoughts flow through our heads continuously. And there are two main categories from which our thoughts arise: the category of Love, and the category of Fear.

The category that our thoughts and actions fall into determines whether we are making functional or dysfunctional choices in life. If we wish to experience a loving, peaceful world, we must choose to think, speak, and act in whichever way supports the category of Love. This is *functional* behaviour. However, if we wish to live in a loving, peaceful world but choose to think, speak, and act in ways which support the category of Fear, we are making *dysfunctional* choices. Since we all desire peace and harmony yet our world is in a state of chaos, I can conclude that humanity has been making dysfunctional choices.

In order to bring Heaven to Earth, each and every one of us must accept responsibility for the state of our planet and begin to make functional choices. We must also accept and BELIEVE that we all have the power to create this new reality—after all, we are only limited by our beliefs. I believe that most people would act with the dignity and courage needed to create a better world *if they believed in their own power!* All they need, then, is a "map" of some kind to guide them on their journey.

Each and every one of us is already endowed with an internal map or guidance system, but many just don't recognize it. This map can be accessed through serious study, meditation, and learning to drop into our heart space.

We are not ALONE – We are ALL ONE!

As stated earlier, one crucial key to finding our true power is to open ourselves to the distinct possibility that we are *not* separate from each other, or from our Source. This false belief of separation is at the root of our problems. Instead, we must open to the knowledge that WE ARE ALL ONE!

When we focus on our differences, causing separation from each other, we empower darkness in our minds and hearts. Once we come to the realization that we are not separate—that we are one—we will, as a species, naturally focus on those aspects of humanity which we hold in common, such as the desire for peace, love, and freedom of choice. We will then begin to make the shift from a dysfunctional world to a functional one.

In truth, we are not as isolated as we believe. We are indeed different, but we are not separate! Our thoughts and energy can be shared through a bond that exists between us—an unseen web that unites us all. In the end, what we are seeking is not the riches of the world, but rather the richness of our soul, and this can only come from realizing that we are connected and whole.

Let's celebrate our differences by utilizing the strengths of each individual and working together as one spirit. We are all endowed with our individual gifts and talents, and every one of us has the power to initiate change—first in ourselves and then coming together as one spirit to ensure the continuation of the human story.

We never walk alone! Even when we waver, we are loved and supported by Divine Source. All seeming coincidences in life are really scenarios to train and strengthen the Peaceful Warrior which resides within every one of us. Our responsibility is to recognize that HOPE is the enemy of despair. Once we realize that we are one, hope enters and negative energy diminishes.

We are at a critical junction. Earth and all who inhabit her are in the midst of the re-birthing of a new humanity. We are entering a new age, a new reality in which we can no longer afford to ignore the song calling out for love. It's time to consciously unplug our ears and repair the damage that we have done so that we can all move forward toward a better future.

Drawing by author.

2

RE-MEMBER

For some, it may be hard to understand this concept of all being connected and how it relates to our lives, both here on Earth and beyond. To understand this better, you can visualize the image of a snow cloud to represent Source (God). Each individual here on Earth comes from that Divine Source, like snowflakes falling to the ground and forming a snowbank.

Just as each snowflake is stamped with its own unique pattern, we humans are each gifted with our own free will. However, our actions and thoughts all come together to form our collective experiences. When we die, we then go through the stages of re-birthing back into Source and returning "home," in the same way that a snowflake melts and eventually returns to the sky.

The purpose of our time on this earthly plane is to make our choices, have (and hopefully enjoy) our experiences, and then return to share these gathered experiences with Source and participate in the evolutionary process of the Divine Universe. This means that while each individual takes on their own unique role in this life, we are all connected as part of this eternal, purposeful cycle.

Automatic drawing by author.

We are all spiritual beings who have chosen to inhabit our own particular human forms as vehicles to experience life on this earthly plane. To live our lives honestly and creatively is to live as humans expressing and becoming our *true* selves.

Drawing by author.

An ancient definition of the word remember is "to put back that which is broken . . . to heal ourselves." As newborns, we assimilate into this physical plane and "forget." Forgetting where we came from and who we really are is a natural phenomenon. To be human is to experience the chaos and trappings of the ego; these are the shackles that bind us. We are broken in spirit because in our heads (which are the sources of our false beliefs), we have created a separation between ourselves and all others, including the Divine Universe of which we are a part. But when we allow ourselves to surrender our human egos and connect with the Universe, we start to "re-member."

In our struggle to release ourselves from this bondage, there exists the *possibility* that we can attain an awareness of our higher selves. This awareness is our key to freedom and helps us ascend to a higher level of consciousness. Awareness of the existence of our higher selves sparks the important process of re-membering or self-healing. And as we begin this healing process of putting ourselves back together, the wings of the Peaceful Warrior within begin to sprout. These wings lift us above the chaos and provide a fresh view of our role here on Earth.

To achieve this, we must remember that we are all energy. We project and receive energy through our thoughts, which then form our reality. The Universe is made of energy, and we are all part of it. This means we each play roles in creating the reality of this Universe, both for ourselves and for others.

Our minds hunger for peace and our hearts thirst for love, but to bring these things into the world, we must begin by leading through personal example. If we start by finding harmony within ourselves, then harmony with the environment (alleviation of our environmental crisis) and harmony with others (easing of our social, political, and economic difficulties) will follow. Actions speak more honestly than words, so the way in which we lead our own lives is the best message we can send to others.

Automatic drawing by author.

Beliefs

--- Go forth toward faith in
self discovery --- notice
all things energetic &
powerful for earth's conflict
with earth's core belief systems ---
clear your
thoughts and proceed to
your goal ---
no negativity will do ---

It is my current belief that there is divine order in ALL things. All that is necessary to bring Heaven to Earth is present, but it will not appear until we collectively decide to raise our energy frequency and open the eyes of our hearts, which are the way we connect to our souls. When we are in our heart, we are connected with our soul at a level deep enough to bring about personal change. We can become productive, compassionate, loving human beings, committed to finding the good in this world and concerned about the feelings of all others.

The challenge in raising this frequency comes from the battle between our higher selves and our egos. Our mental and emotional states are two forms of energy vibrations, and the ego attempts to control these two states in order to create a separation between them and our higher selves—and most of the time, it succeeds. When the ego is in control, our energy is negative and dense, keeping us in the dark ages.

In contrast, when our higher selves are in control of our mental and emotional states, we have positive spiritual experiences that lead us to a higher level of energy vibration.

If what we desire is a world living in peace and harmony, we need to change our behaviours. However, we cannot make a long-term change in our behaviours without addressing the beliefs that underlie them. Change is triggered through the power of thought, not action, because thought produces action. We humans do the same thing over and over again because we have not changed our basic beliefs—about Source and about life. We must change our beliefs before we can change our actions.

To truly embrace the understanding that we are all one, we need to recognize that God (Source) and life are one and the same. Source is what life is, and life is what Source is. Source is the energy we call life, and life is the energy that we call Source. Life is the Divine Source (God), manifested in this physical world. It's all the same thing. Everything is connected; WE are connected. We are all one, and we must work together to shed our egos and achieve a higher vibration.

Go Deep

In nature, fish intuitively know to dive to deeper, calmer waters when there is a storm or if the weather is too hot. Likewise, we humans naturally come to the waves at the surface in order to feed ourselves with experiences, but we should always stay centred in the deep stillness of love and compassion. We can learn to ride the waves of life—the ups and downs—like a bubble, but we must keep in mind that life is calmer and more stable at the deep end of the ocean. If we continually strive for and study love in action, we create a deeper ocean for ourselves and become more stable at our core.

Of course, nobody is perfect—there is no such thing. There will be times when we spend too long on the surface, caught up in the events of the world and ignoring our inner guidance. But as long as we don't get stuck at the surface, we will continue to grow spiritually.

Accessing this part of ourselves is an important skill to learn because the world around us is a mirror of what we have become. So, if we wish to see change in our world, we must become that change in our everyday lives. If we wish for peace, tolerance, and compassion at the global level, we must become that. If we'd like to see a collaborative change, we must individually *become* that change. And the only way to achieve this is to spend time in those deeper waters, listening for our higher selves and learning from all we have experienced.

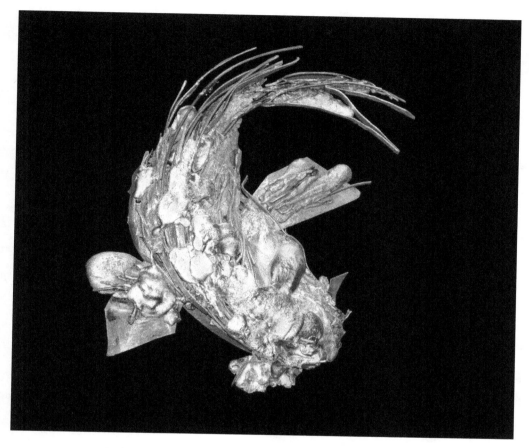

Sculpture by author using metal, wire, and solder, titled "Go deep."

Illusion versus Truth

Life is like a magic show, and we often get caught up in the illusion, believing that this world is real and unchangeable. But no matter what we say, do, or believe, the truth never changes—that this reality is a projection of our thoughts and that we have full control over what it looks like. Nothing can mask this truth. So why is the truth always so hard for us to see and understand? Shouldn't this be simple? Perhaps this is nature's method of allowing us to experience a full range of emotions—to experience falsehood so we have the opportunity to recognize reality.

A simple example of illusion masking the truth can be found in a roadrunner battling a rattlesnake. The roadrunner depends on speed and illusion to defeat the snake. It fakes with its tail and wings, then attacks quickly from various angles while the snake (who is unable to see the truth in the roadrunner's actions) is baffled. This is just like our egos hiding the truth from us, using illusion to keep us confused and continue our separation from the world around us.

Many times, though, when we do glimpse the truth, we hesitate to act upon it. This is because we have been taught false beliefs for many years, handing them down from generation to generation. If we act on our new understandings of life, we feel disloyal to our upbringing and to all those who have taught us. We can overcome this guilty feeling by dropping our focus into our hearts and listening to the silent, wise voice within that will guide us toward the truth.

3

ENERGY/CHI

I AM NOTHING.......I AM EVERYTHING

For many years, I enjoyed raising tropical fish as a hobby. I would spend hours just sitting quietly in the room with the lights out, gazing at the life forms swimming about. It was a fairly large tank, so the fish residing at the top level of the tank were relatively oblivious to the existence of the fish at the bottom. However, I noticed that whenever there was a dramatic scuffle or major action at the bottom level, the water would carry the energy of the movements through the tank, making the hapless fish at the top become unsettled—sometimes to the point of causing them to flounder and even panic.

I see this fish tank as an example of how our own energy field works. We humans are similarly surrounded by an ocean of energy. Our thoughts are energy, atoms are energy, food is energy, life is energy. We are all made up of and connected through this energy, and therefore we all have a common bond. This means that disruptions to our energy ripple outward and affect both the world around us and the people within it. So, doesn't it make sense that we should learn to live together harmoniously?

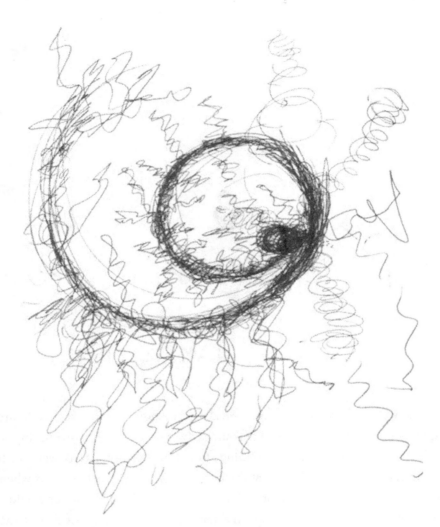

Automatic drawing by author.

All living beings—not just humans—experience a subtle form of vital energy flowing throughout their bodies. There are many names for this energy. In China it is known as *chi*, in Japan it is called *ki*, and in India it is referred to as *prana*. For the sake of simplicity, I will refer to this life force as chi (pronounced "chee").

Chi is the air we breathe and the energy and vitality that sustain us. A living being is filled with chi, but a dead person is not—their life energy is gone. In addition, a healthy individual has more chi than one who is ill, though good health is more than just an abundance of chi. Good health infers that the chi in our bodies is clear rather than tainted or murky, and that it is flowing smoothly like a stream, not congested or stagnant.

Chi is also the life energy one senses in nature. The earth itself is in motion—it is constantly changing, breathing, and alive with chi. When we appreciate the beauty of the animals, birds, trees, mountains, and oceans, we are sensing their chi and feeling a sense of unity with them. We living beings are all part of the great universal chi, and chi is part of every living being.

For thousands of years energy workers, psychics, martial artists, and all others in the healing arts have been accessing and working with this life force. In fact, our whole existence is determined by this energy—our physical, mental, and emotional balances are conditioned by the chi in and around our bodies. Mustering, conserving, and using chi is therefore vital to maintaining an enjoyable and healthy life.

Chi runs through our bodies and flows in channels that are known to acupuncture practitioners, whose main goal is to remove blockages in these channels and promote a smooth flow of energy. Our minds move chi through our bodies and our environment, and this flow is far more efficient when we use a certain degree of concentration or visualization.

We have the power to shift, change, clear, and release energy at any time, which means that everything around us can be manipulated by our energy and intention. So, to be a conscious creator in life, we need *energy awareness*. Many people marginalize themselves by limiting the definition of who they are as nothing more than a physical body. In truth, our physical body is contained within our personal energy field. We aren't just a body that *has* energy; we are conscious energy *being* human.

Through the diligent study and practise of Chi Kung (the research of life energy), we can open our bodies to a balanced, natural flow of chi. We can use Chi Kung as a starting point to understand the workings of the earth, nature, and even ourselves. The training is focused on the subtle internal vitality that energizes us and invigorates all the life support systems of the human body, from the circulation of blood to the health of our muscles, tendons, and internal organs.

Chi Kung training involves calm, regulated breathing; slow, gentle, unforced movements; mental focus or mindfulness; and inner stillness. It is the art of cultivating our breath to promote the smooth circulation of our chi. Rather than retreating from our chaotic outer world, Chi Kung can assist us in getting in touch with what is real and meaningful in our lives. Each of us can bolster peace in our world by creating peace within ourselves. Then, like a small pebble thrown into a pond, ripples of energy expand outward and affect others.

I am grateful to all my teachers of Chi Kung for imparting such valuable knowledge to me. Personally, I have integrated Chi Kung practice into my daily world, not only as part of my martial arts practice but also as a method of maintaining good physical health. Over the years, my personal Chi Kung practice has also gifted me with many spiritual treasures, the most valuable being the gift of a calm, peaceful heart and the awareness of my sacred space within.

For those who are interested in learning more about Chi Kung, there are many good books and CDs available on this subject. However, it is best to learn from a qualified Chi Kung instructor if possible.

4

HUMAN TRUTH

Every human being is an individual with their own fears, doubts, and goals. But one thing is certain: we each have something special about us—a talent we can use to contribute to society. Sometimes, though, this special gift is well-disguised.

When I was in high school, a group of my friends were discussing what they were going to do after graduation. Some were going to attend university while others were pursuing a trade, but they were all pretty sure of their choices.

However, when my friends asked what I had decided to do, I told them that I wasn't sure. They said, "What do you mean, you're not sure?! You're going to be a veterinarian or an artist, aren't you?"

"Well, yes . . . but isn't there something more?"

"What do you mean, 'something more'? Do you want to be famous or something?"

"No, I just have this gnawing feeling that there's something else, something more, but I can't put my finger on it!"

Well, it didn't take long for me to be the butt of everyone's jokes. After all, this was back in the 1960s when nobody openly expressed their feelings—especially men!

I couldn't explain the nagging feeling that there was something more important in life than choosing a profession. I had no idea why I was feeling this way, but I just couldn't shake it.

After graduation, I did become an artist. I also got married and raised my family. However, that gnawing feeling persisted throughout my adulthood. There were many nights when I would lay awake till morning, frustrated and confused by my inability to find the answers to life. Some nights I would manage to fall asleep, only to be jarred awake (usually around 3 a.m.) by some mysterious sound or my own internal alarm clock. Then the nagging thoughts would run their loop in my head until dawn.

Automatic drawing by author.

The first seeds of my many nagging questions, along with the answers I was searching for, were actually planted many years before. When I was about seven years old, Dad took me to visit the Chinese Athletic Hall where he and his brothers studied Kung Fu in their youth. I was just a young kid then, but I remember my dad introducing me to a friendly old man who asked me many questions about myself, then showed me the ancient armour and weapons that were stored in a huge closet. I remember him leading me by the hand into the small storage space and how the sight of it all mesmerized me. The aroma from the armour permeated my nostrils and worked its way into my body. The old man told me in Cantonese that this belonged to me—that the heritage was mine. Perhaps my young mind subconsciously held on to his words and gave them some kind of magical meaning. Perhaps not. What this experience did instill was a sense of wonderment about my ancestry, along with a sense of belonging to a martial arts community.

This visit came when I was at a young, impressionable age, and it set the stage for a life of questioning and searching for answers. Somehow, the aroma and sight of the armour and weapons stirred something within me—an inner recognition of sorts. My dad obviously respected the old man, so I looked to him as some type of wizard and took his words seriously. I wondered what he meant by telling me that this belonged to me; did he mean the armour and weapons, or did he mean martial arts? I was too young to delve deeply into these questions at the time, but they remained with me throughout my life.

Over the years, the leaves covering my spiritual path were blown aside through my training in martial arts and Chi Kung, with each overturned leaf revealing a bit more of the truth. My training, combined with lessons learned through animal communication sessions, gradually brought me to a point where I'm now consciously aware of my personal duty to hang on to my Human Truth in all circumstances and situations—to study, persevere, try, endure. I must consider others with unconditional love, and every action I take must shine with spirit from my heart. I must trust my intuition!

Automatic drawing by author.

Was this visit to the Chinese Athletic Hall a scripted part of my life? It sure feels like it. In fact, throughout my life, some unseen force has come along when I least expected it and nudged me toward the truth—coaxing me patiently, allowing me to take time in maturing and learning. And along the way, special people, animals, and situations crossed my path, each one shedding a little more light into the darkness and helping me find my Human Truth—my path or way.

If you cease to try, you cease to exist!

My Human Truth

Years ago, while I was in a deep state of meditation, a mysterious inner voice came through with this personal message: "I must be-come that which I am." Because I was in this higher state of being at the time, I naturally understood the meaning of this statement. The inner voice repeated these words over and over, likely to imbed the words and their meaning in my mind.

However, the constant repetition of these words took me out of that higher state, and I then lost my understanding of them. The inner voice coaxed my logical thinking mind to repeat these words, but the more I repeated them, the less I understood them. The inner voice eventually dissipated, and my logical mind was left to repeat these words, which by now had lost all meaning, alone.

I immediately wrote the words down on a piece of paper and tried to recall their mysterious meaning, but to no avail. I knew that this was an important piece of information, so I went over it again and again, repeating the words as a mantra.

Over time, I finally arrived at my own personal interpretation of the words. I must come to be the highest version of my self—in other words, I must come to be the manifestation of my higher self (my God presence). These words have become an important reminder for myself and an integral part of my daily spiritual practice.

Each of us has our own Human Truth within us—our own path—and once it's discovered, we cannot go backwards. Instead, we have the choice to either live our Truth or to deny it and live in the world of illusion.

My Human Truth is simply this: to give strength and spirit to all those around me, to be a positive influence in their lives, and to leave a positive legacy for the following generations. And I hope this Truth will help you find your own way.

When I'm ready – I will BE

Peaceful Warrior Arts

Peaceful Warrior Arts logo, by author.

Many years ago, I sat down to design myself a logo which would serve to convey my personal Truths. Within this logo are two facets. One facet represents the side view of a human figure bowing in respect—hands touching the ground with knees bent. In my martial arts classes, this bowing posture portrays the loving respect one has for another's highest potential.

The other facet portrays humans as a microcosm of the Universe—of the natural world. The head (shown in grey) represents the sun and moon. The shoulder, back, and arm represent a mountain. The bent legs represent the earth, and the space between the thigh and lower leg represents water.

Everything in nature is interdependent and works in harmony, just like how we humans are interdependent on each other. We are like individual cells in the same body: what is good for a lung cell is good for a liver cell, and what is detrimental to a heart cell is detrimental to a kidney cell. We are different, but we are not separate. We are ONE.

If it is true that we are a microcosm of the Universe, then clearly we are one with the Universe and with each other. The Universe consists of positive and negative forces, as are humans. We all have positive and negative attributes, which are not polar opposites, but rather complementary forces. The trick is to be capable of balancing these two forces within ourselves—NOT by refusing to acknowledge that we all have "bad" qualities, but by acknowledging the good and the bad, then finding a balance. This holds true for our physical body (health) as well as our mind (characteristics).

Together, these two facets of my logo represent two of my strongest beliefs: that we are all connected and that we are destined to become our higher selves. I use this logo in many circumstances.

The Warrior Within

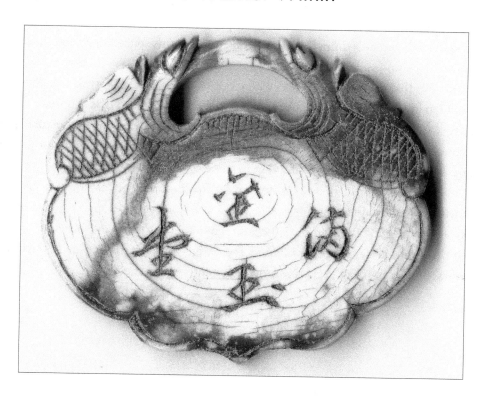

This amulet has accompanied the author since infancy.

When I was born in 1946, Mr. Menzies—the curator of the Vancouver Museum at the time and a dear friend of my parents—brought me an amulet carved from bone, which he found during one of his many excursions into the jungles of China and India.

Both sides are inscribed with Chinese characters. The characters on the flip side (not shown) roughly translate as follows: LONG – LIFE – PROSPEROUS – WEALTHY. So, one could consider this amulet to be typically used as a good luck charm. The characters on the side shown roughly translate as follows: PRECIOUS – JADE/EMERALD – FULL/OVERFLOW – HALL/SPACE. These words could be taken as an additional blessing for the recipient to receive a bounty of material wealth (a huge room overflowing with precious gems).

However, my father once shared with me his personal take on this inscription. He believed that this amulet also carries a subtle but empowering message for those who are willing to dig a bit deeper: that a sacred space exists within every one of us, and if we have the will and determination to seek out and find this space, we will connect with something far more valuable and precious than material wealth.

I believe that this sacred space is where our powerful Inner Warrior lies dormant, the seed having been planted by the thumb of the Divine Source. The moment we discover this space and consent to the nurturing of our Inner Warrior, a spiritual spark is generated and the seed begins to emerge and grow. Each seed develops in its own unique way, and each has the potential to become a Warrior for Peace.

A true Peaceful Warrior is one who walks softly on this Earth, balancing a peaceful heart with a warrior's fighting spirit. A Peaceful Warrior dedicates their life to a higher purpose of service to others and has the courage to follow their own heart.

If this message resonates with you, I encourage you to start your own journey of discovery, possibly through self-study, deep pondering, and meditation.

so – much is to be said
& done for love to arrive safely
– may you strengthen
& polish the warrior within so
power / love can flow outwards

Am I Trying?

If there is one thing we humans all have in common, regardless of our station in life, it is that we are each gifted with free will and are able to choose whether or not to TRY.

Years ago, when my daughters were in their teens, one of their friends received a new car from her parents as a reward for getting good grades in school. So, I approached my daughters to talk about their expectations. I told them that I loved them and was proud of them both for having done well throughout their school years. I then asked them if they felt unloved or cheated when they didn't receive such grandiose gifts. I was happy, but not surprised, when they both told me that they knew I loved them, and that they knew I would be proud of them no matter what grades they received. They said that no extravagant gifts were necessary, or even desired.

In response, I told them that the one thing of *real* value I could give them was a promise to honestly try my best in life. By watching me throughout the coming years, they'll see for themselves whether I've kept my promise by persevering and trying—or not! Then, maybe they can learn from this. Hopefully, they'll learn that as long as you make an honest effort, nothing can ever stop you from attaining happiness and a calm heart.

Question: Am I walking the right path?

Answer: Yes – although a little crooked.

I believe we are all in this Earth school to experience, learn, and re-member that we are here to uncover our purpose in life. Once we uncover our purpose, our soul's journey then becomes a path to fulfilling our destiny.

It's tough to find your path in life. And once you find it, you need courage and endurance to follow your way, undeterred by anything except your inner guidance—although consideration must be given to all others. It takes a strong spirit to constantly balance all areas of your life while remaining true to your path, but remember that there are unseen forces supporting you, and that you are never, EVER alone.

Part 2

MARTIAL ARTS FOR PEACE

Automatic drawing by author.

5

A LIFETIME OF LESSONS

"How many people can you kill?"

Throughout the 1970s and 1980s, people often asked me this question after finding out that I was involved in martial arts. This revealed a common, distorted viewpoint about those who were engaged in this study. I haven't been asked this question recently, so I'm hopeful that this mindset is changing for the better.

I was a young boy when Kung Fu first caught my attention; I'm now in my mid-to-late-seventies and still appreciative of the benefits of martial arts training. Most of my life has been formed around the study and teaching of martial arts and its related fields (Karate-Do, Kung Fu, Chi Kung, energy healing, acupressure, and more). The seed was planted so many years ago that I now feel the need to reflect—to ask myself if all these years in the martial arts has been of any value. Have I managed to harness it as my vehicle for personal growth? Will I be able to leave a legacy for the younger generation? Have I gleaned anything of value through my training in martial arts—anything worthy enough to affect their lives in a positive way?

wield the sword of righteousness

One particular question played on my mind: Have I taught anything of lasting value to my students? Then, one special day, I looked in the mirror and became aware that *I* was my only student! *I* was the one with the responsibility to change and grow! Others could share this journey with me if they wished, but they were responsible for their own growth as well.

In 1971, Sensei Tomoaki Koyabu was sent from Japan by Kaicho Seikichi Toguchi to introduce Okinawan Goju Ryu Shorei-Kan Karate-Do to Canada. I had the pleasure of being introduced to him by a mutual friend, and we began training together in my sister's basement. Sensei Koyabu had to return to Japan while awaiting immigration papers and then returned to Canada in early 1972, when we started our first Karate dojo in Canada. Sensei Koyabu was a young man who couldn't speak English, so it took tremendous courage on his part to move to Canada in pursuit of his life's goal. We became close friends, but I will always look to him as my teacher and the Canadian master.

During one conversation I had with Sensei Koyabu, I asked if he was frustrated or disappointed that there was a constant turnover of students, with not many pursuing martial arts as a serious study. He replied, "You can lead a horse to water, but you can't make it drink!"

On another occasion, Sensei Koyabu and I were gardening together, and our conversation turned to the parallels between our Karate training and our daily lives. He pointed to one of the large maple trees in the yard and commented that this tree was a healthy specimen, each branch playing a role in its overall health by reaching skyward for the sun's nutrition. This was nature in harmony. If these branches began to turn in on themselves, the branches would intertwine and eventually choke each other, killing the tree. Likewise, if each member of a family works in harmony and balance with their siblings and parents, the family unit will grow strong and healthy. If the family members turned against each other with negative thoughts and actions, the family will falter and become dysfunctional.

Our conversation then turned to one of the advanced Karate kata (a solo form for practising techniques like blocks, punches, and timing). One unique defensive feature of this particular kata is the dismantling of an opponent's attack, starting at his extremities and working toward his centre to upset his balance. Sensei Koyabu called my attention to a massive bush, covered with sharp thorns, that needed pruning. He told me if he tried to go straight to the centre of this bush, he would be torn to ribbons by all the thorns. Instead, he began at the outer edges and methodically worked his way toward the centre by trimming the branches and thorns from their extremities, one by one. In a short time, he had the bush pruned to perfection—and he did it without suffering one scratch. He harnessed the concepts from the Karate kata and demonstrated its practical applications in daily life.

I have always valued Sensei Koyabu's wise teachings, and I have put them to good use many times in my personal life.

Automatic drawing by author.

In martial arts, we are taught that change is the only constant. If a concept or technique is dysfunctional (meaning it doesn't work), you study it, find out where and why it's inefficient, then implement some kind of change so that it becomes functional. This truth can also be applied to our daily lives.

My definition of the term kata (or martial arts solo form) is who you are at that precise moment in time and space. Therefore, performing kata is training yourself to "be." The practice of kata requires mindfulness throughout the time it takes to perform it, so you are training yourself to be mindful and live in the present—not focusing on what comes before or after, but what is happening NOW.

The concentration required for this practice calms the mind. It is said that form is captivity, and the loss of form is freedom—but before we can become *free*, we must understand or experience *captivity*. So, we must study our kata, our style, and then grow by losing our form and becoming creative individuals, training with the awareness that we must avoid becoming imprisoned—that we must go beyond. Likewise, in our daily lives, we should be wary of becoming imprisoned within our old, false belief systems which restrict and separate us.

In martial arts, concentrating on technique alone is hollow, leaving you with a shallow foundation. Those who rely solely on technique are easily uprooted and are limited to only what they have memorized. In contrast, being grounded in and knowledgeable about the important concepts allows for versatility, true strength, unlimited techniques, and more. Currently, our society seeks to change itself using "techniques" (laws, rules, and regulations) without addressing the root causes of the problems and chaos we are experiencing: our beliefs. If we want to make lasting change, we need to go back to the basics and build up our spiritual foundation.

It's also important to remember that even though we are all connected, we are all on our own personal paths. There's a martial arts saying that goes, "No second-hand Karate—own it! Make it your own!" Likewise, we must not follow others blindly as we move through life. Instead, we should explore the depths of our play and discover who we truly are at our core.

Glass frit art by author, titled "Pondering the Martial Arts Path."

6

LESSONS FROM MY MENTORS

Dad – My First Teacher

With his fingers forming a crane's beak, Dad simultaneously struck downwards behind himself while thrusting one knee upwards, balancing on one leg and shouting "Dohk!" I remember this moment so clearly—I was captivated as I watched my father transform his personal space while performing his Kung Fu.

It was the early 1950s—a challenging time for my dad. He was a proud, gentle Chinese man, born and raised in Canada, and he found himself frustrated and bound by a prejudiced society. However, he was able to find his inner strength, his true self, while performing his Chinese Kung Fu forms (also known as "kata" in Okinawan Karate). The term "form" refers to a detailed choreographed pattern of punches, kicks, blocks, and stances designed for solo practice. This simulates actual fighting situations and allows the practitioner to develop timing as well as a fighting spirit.

Dad's display of intensity, focus, and power mesmerized me. It was in these moments that I could see the balance between his chaotic outer world and his calm inner world. There was something immeasurable and indescribable here—a spark of energy which affected me for life.

At the time, I was a seven-year-old Chinese Canadian boy who got into fights while defending myself and others from those who used racist slurs and prejudice against us. I was interested in learning Dad's Kung Fu and asked him to teach me, but he told me that Kung Fu was "special"—something to be studied seriously and only used for protection. I argued my case, telling him that I had good reason to learn because a lot of my fights were centred around protecting my friend Akira, a mentally challenged Japanese boy who was constantly being picked on by bullies.

Dad eventually agreed to teach me and allowed me to watch him, but only if I promised not to talk or ask unnecessary questions. He was very secretive and would never display his skills in public, so I watched him in the unlit privacy of his bedroom or our little parlour. I would examine Dad's movements and listen intensely to his breathing, grabbing any little bit of information I could. However, he only gave me glimpses, seldom repeating his moves or spending too much time on explanations. He just advised me to watch, study, and copy.

What I sensed while my father was performing his Kung Fu was honesty and integrity. He displayed mindfulness and expressed who he was at that particular moment in time. He wasn't dwelling in the past or fretting about the future; he was, in that moment, calm and at peace. The spark in Dad's eyes while practising came from his heart—from his spirit communicating with a higher source of power. This was just a glimmer of the tip of the iceberg, and I felt it was my duty to get under the surface to find the real treasures hidden there.

Now that I am in the autumn of my life, I ponder the impact my father had on me. He had one foot in his Chinese heritage and the other in Western culture, and he struggled to achieve some level of balance. He would relate many stories and parables of olden China, but he also taught me to be proud of and grateful for having Canada as my home country. As a young impressionable boy, these stories would take on a flavour, a smell, an essence, instilling in me the belief that there was some type of mysterious power that was greater than us human beings. And somehow, Kung Fu was allowing Dad to communicate with this power.

What little I managed to capture with my young eyes fuelled my hunger. I couldn't verbalize what it was that I sensed in my father's Kung Fu, but it has probably been the driving force throughout all these years of my own martial arts study.

I am fortunate to have been influenced by my father's Kung Fu and the high value he placed on it. His philosophy of integrity, gentleness, and kindness were linked to his Kung Fu and steeped in tradition. His upbringing and cultural training influenced his attitude toward sharing it with me. His Kung Fu was his sacred place, and I'm forever grateful that he took me along for the ride.

Explore the Depths of Our Play

In 1990, my friend Sensei Hirakawa, chief instructor of Southern Japan, invited me to fly to Japan to take part in the opening ceremonies of his new Karate dojo. Along the way, I stopped off in Tokyo to visit with Karate master Kaicho Seikichi Toguchi and his wife Halukosan. We talked for hours. Kaicho encouraged me to step out on my own and create a new branch on our Karate family tree for the benefit of society.

I told him I had little confidence that society could gain any benefit from me—what did I have that society would want or need? In response, Kaicho pointed to his heart and said, "Kokoro!" (heart/mind/soul connection).

He then grabbed a thick Karate magazine. He didn't open it though. Instead, he flipped it over so that I could see the back cover, which was a full-page ad for a pen company. It read something like: "Of all you can write throughout the years of your life, what, if anything, is worthy of presenting to the next generation?"

Kaicho told me that nothing in the Karate magazine, which focused strictly on the sports aspect, was worth reading—that only this advertisement held anything of value for me. He encouraged me to walk my own path—to put brush to canvas and create from my heart.

That was not the only time Kaicho Toguchi gave me some wise advice. He was the one who suggested I teach and share mainly lessons learned through my own life experiences and advised me not to rely on the words of others to find my own personal

Human Truths. He also explained that there are three levels of martial arts teachers:

1. the many, who are walking the established pathway;
2. the fewer, who take the path less travelled; and
3. the handful, who do not take any trail or path which has been forged by others, choosing instead to walk through a swamp.

Kaicho suggested that I, like him, will choose the swamp. He also said to be prepared because when I turn around to see who is accompanying me, I will find myself alone. Nobody—no student, friend, or family member—will accompany me.

At the time, I couldn't grasp the truth in what he said to me. But as I look back now, I realize that he was teaching me about life. We are each responsible for our own journey in life, and we cannot expect others to commit themselves to our path, no matter how much they may love or believe in us.

listen – hear us calling from
around you – we say this to
you now – come and stand up
for all – now is now –
waiting is for fools not for heroes –
call upon our hearts
wings beating flowing in
harmonious sounds
so ears to hear may hear to act –
act with faith!!

7

DY AND HIS DO

In Japan, the word *Do* (pronounced "dough") stands for art as a body of knowledge, principles, and techniques pursued for the perfection of the human spirit. In martial arts, it is used to describe a way or path to spiritual understanding and self-realization. Do is used after the word Karate as a direct translation of the Chinese word *Tao* (the way).

The highest aspiration of the martial arts is that they should be the "arts of peace," pursued through a way of harmony with the Universal Spirit. The key to unlocking this spirit is to understand the universality of chi and to respect and sustain it in ourselves and in others.

Throughout the years, my friend DY would ask me, "Why do you say Karate-Do? Why not just say Karate? And what does Do mean anyway? I don't get it!"

I would explain that "Karate" translated to empty hand and "Do" stood for "the way" or "the path," so together they become "the way of the empty hand." However, I could never explain the concept clearly enough for him to fully digest the information. So, DY would simply respond with a confused grin and a shrug of his shoulders.

On DY's fiftieth birthday, I wrote him this letter in an attempt to explain his personal connection to the word Karate-Do.

DY -

Karate-Do translates as the way of the empty hand.
When we're born, we're born alone and with empty hands.
When we die, we die alone and with empty hands.

The time spent between these two events is usually concerned
with gathering and filling our hands—most of us not realizing
that these possessions are only temporary and placing excessive value on
them.

DY, you keep your hands busy with tools—usually to work on projects for
other people. There's a belief that what a man does reflects his true self (i.e.,
actions speak louder than words).

Further to that belief, "If you bow, bow low" means that any kind action
must be backed by sincere intentions or it is a hollow act.

You told me that you help people with their projects for yourself—because
YOU enjoy doing it, not necessarily just to please them or just to be a nice
guy. And that's the point—you are sincerely happy being yourself, usually in
the service of others.

You don't NEED anything—no big payment, no reward, no praise.
This is your Way. This is your Karate-Do.

We can all learn to apply the concept of Karate-Do in our lives. Through meditation, dropping into our heart space, and deep pondering, we can each uncover our own special talents to be of service to others. What it takes to begin this journey is to practise being in a state of gratitude and to place attention on your higher purpose.

8

WHAT THE MARTIAL ARTS TEACH US

The key aspects of martial arts are also the key aspects of life. I don't expect you to head out and begin practising martial arts just to experience these teachings for yourselves, though, so I'm passing along some lessons I've learned so that you can apply them to your own life.

Flexibility and Change

In martial arts, rigidity in thought or movement restricts our fighting ability. So, we always strive to create flexibility in our bodies through exercises, stretching, and movement in order to achieve the maximum range of motion. We also use kata, meditation, and theory to build flexibility in our minds.

Similarly, if we take a rigid approach to our lives, we close our minds to the opinions and ideas of others and the truth becomes harder to see clearly. However, if we continually strive for flexibility, we train ourselves to stay open to the ideas and opinions of others, making life a lot easier for those around us as well as for ourselves.

Nature works in harmony and balance as yin and yang forces complement each other. Energy is always in motion and moves in circles (what goes around, comes around). To see the truth in this statement, you only need to look at the natural world around you: morning transforms into day, and day into night; leaves on a tree bud, then blossom and eventually fall off; shorelines slowly erode from the movements of the water; seasons with heat eventually turn to cold; old trees die and fall to the earth, creating new life. We are a microcosm of nature, so we all benefit from studying its workings and modelling our thoughts and actions off the knowledge we gain from this study.

Cut paper art by author, titled "Change Is the Only Constant."
(Note that the shadows on the uniform take on the form of trees/nature.)

As an example, in martial arts there is a stance called "shikodachi" (named horse stance because the practitioner appears to be riding a horse). The shikodachi stance is strong and stable, appearing unmovable and static. However, change is the only constant in marital arts, just like in life. Our weight is never stagnant—we try not to become "double-weighted" in our stances or during transitions. One foot is always yin, the other is yang. We never stick to one position, and we always anticipate that our attacker will try to surprise us. So, shikodachi is actually a transition movement in which yin and yang forces are in action. Energy is subtly shifted back and forth from one foot to the other, creating true fluid balance.

Change is also the only "constant" in our daily lives. We can never stay the same; our lives never stay as they are. So, in order to get the most out of our time here on Earth, we must be open to change and take advantage of our awareness of it.

Yielding with Strength

In martial arts, using our attacker's force against them through body positioning, lateral movement, and other yielding methods is extremely effective. For example, when a strong attacker uses his arms to push against your upper body, rather than push back, you can step back with one foot and reposition your hips and torso with a yielding motion—like a swinging gate. This allows your attacker to continue his momentum by falling forward, thus creating an opening in his defences which we can fill.

This same concept holds true in our daily lives. If we are verbally accosted by aggression, we will not attain harmony by retaliating with more aggression. Instead, we must remain as centred as possible and sidestep to redirect the verbal assault. This allows us to look at the overall situation from a more peaceful vantage point.

One of my martial arts students was an art director for a large ad agency that held regularly scheduled meetings to discuss various projects. My student confided in me that his coworkers were making aggressive comments during these meetings, and that it was causing him stress. To combat this, I suggested that he examine the physics behind our chest blocks. We don't try to match our strength with the strength of our attacker. Instead, we deflect his punch while stepping slightly to the side, facing his centre. From this vantage point, we are able to assess our situation. I suggested that he try this technique in the boardroom, deflecting the negative comments aimed at him by taking a deep breath; responding to those comments with confidence, non-aggressiveness, and openness; and then mentally stepping aside to face his aggressor with calmness and peacefulness. He was excited to begin implementing his newfound defensive strategy right away. When someone approached him with verbal aggression, he would verbally deflect these attacks with success.

About a year later, my student showed me a letter from his bosses congratulating him for changing his attitude and becoming a team player. Clearly, this new approach had allowed him to communicate with his coworkers in a more meaningful way.

Standing Our Ground

During a physical assault, determination is key—once our mind loses its determination, we take on a victim or loser mentality and therefore become victims. As the saying goes, "The worst opponent is one whose aim has become an obsession." So, once we decide to stand our ground and fight, we must be sincere in that decision and fight wholeheartedly until the end. We must believe that we will not be a victim. We must be fierce but have patience at the same time so that we can outlast our attacker. And most importantly, we must have complete determination.

Good character, total truth, and sincerity can also be developed by standing our ground when necessary. In order to progress on our spiritual journey, we must be honest (both with ourselves and with others) and always head for the truth. We can't accept falseness or treat illusions as reality.

Happiness Training

"What would *really* make you happy?"

During my time as a young adult, this is a question I would often pose to people I met at various functions. To define my question further, I would add, "I don't mean winning the lottery or becoming famous—nothing like that. If your doctor told you that you had only so long to live, what would give you a sense that your life is 'right'?"

Most people were taken aback and found it difficult to respond immediately—and naturally so. The search for true happiness is one of our primary human instincts, and each of us has our own definition of this word. So, determining what would make us happy is challenging because there is no one right answer we can turn to.

Regardless of the individual responses to my question, I believe that the path to true happiness begins with a calm mind and spirit. After all, a calm, peaceful mind affects our total well-being—both physical and mental.

Many artists incorporate Chinese characters into their ornamental designs to help bring us happiness and longevity. The old Chinese symbol for happiness (generally referring to marital happiness) is called Double Happiness, made up of two of the characters that translate to joy. From my personal martial arts perspective, the ideogram Double Happiness conveys *all* that naturally results when complementary forces such as male/female, intention/action, yin/yang, Heaven/Earth, and mind/body work in harmony. The Universe moves in perfect balance, and as humans are a microcosm of the Universe, the same natural laws relate to us.

For instance, while cycling, everyone knows that when the left leg takes action (yang), the right leg gets to rest (yin), and vice versa. The result, of course, is a harmony of forces. There is no conflict.

Any relationship which acts in accord with the laws of nature creates a state of happiness—or in this case, Double Happiness. However, due to these chaotic, troubled times we live in—and due to the false sense of separation we have created between each other and our Divine Source—happiness seems to be quite elusive.

So, how can martial arts incorporate the training of not only mind but also body and spirit in order to put us on the road to happiness?

- Mind training: utilizing the principles of yin and yang.
- Body training: incorporating Chi Kung training into our regime to learn at a physical level how to balance our energy flow, which helps our minds relax.
- Spiritual training: practising meditation.

Through these practices, we learn to balance our emotions in order to guide us toward happiness and peace. For example, if anger is yang, then love is yin. Both yin and yang must be in balance. If we have too much anger, we can balance it by reducing anger and adding love.

It's natural to have feelings of anger and to need to vent our emotions—that's healthy. But if we are not balanced, we will carry our anger to extremes that result in hatred, grudges, physical violence, and more, which of course becomes a negative influence on society as a whole. To combat this, we can take the holistic point of view to help train ourselves. Rather than focus on just our wants, we step back and look at how our actions and thoughts will affect the world around us.

All of the practices in this chapter take time, effort, and determination to incorporate into our daily lives. However, the outcome is worth it. By embracing these ideas, we can bring more peace into our lives and move closer to our higher selves.

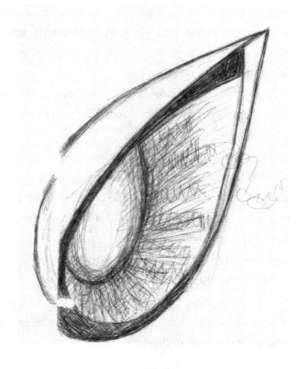

Automatic drawing by author.

9

THE MOUNTAIN

Mountains are often referred to in the martial arts as an image to visualize when relating parables for spiritual growth. In this particular instance, the mountain became more: it became the setting for a life-defining experience.

For much of my adult life, I was a spiritual fence-sitter—always leaning toward searching for Truth but not committing to it. My experience on the mountain was the pivotal event which knocked me off the fence. It was my defining life experience—my seminal event.

October 30, 1994, started out as any other day. Then, we received a phone call from our friend Leigh telling us that her mother-in-law, Bachan (the Japanese term for grandmother), was lost somewhere on Blackcomb Mountain, near the skiing town of Whistler, BC. She had been mushroom picking with her eldest son and had somehow wandered off. Many people had been called in to look for her, including the local search and rescue team. However, it was a dangerous situation as a blinding snowstorm had rolled in and visibility had become extremely poor.

I immediately offered to drive up to the mountain to join in the search, but Leigh asked me to stay put for a while. They already had a lot of volunteers, and she felt that it would be advantageous to have me wait in Vancouver in case they needed me to bring supplies up later. Sure enough, she called again late in the afternoon and asked if I would drive to their house to pick up supplies. Her husband, Terry, planned to meet his brother Ted and me at the foot of the mountain with his 4x4, and we'd all head back up to join the search.

My daughters were determined that I should stay home. They knew I would take risks in order to find Bachan, and they begged me to stay home, fearing for my safety. They reminded me of my fear of the dark and my habit of getting lost. When I said that I had no choice but to go, my older daughter said that she was coming along to protect me. However, I felt it was much too dangerous for her. We argued for a while until I finally put my foot down and left. (She had a dream later that night which showed Terry and me standing waist deep in water, crying. I now believe that it was a premonition for what was to come.)

I drove to Leigh's house, loaded some supplies into my car, and headed for Blackcomb. At 10:45 p.m., I was passing through the Stanley Park Causeway and some sort of energy pulled my eyes to the right, directing my attention to the small section of water by the Vancouver Yacht Club. My hair stood on end, and I became very upset and had to choke back tears. This baffled me, but I reasoned that the stress of Bachan's situation was getting the best of me.

Terry met Ted and me at the base of the mountain. We transferred the supplies into his 4x4 and left my car parked there before heading back up the mountain to the base camp. The search had been discontinued for the night due to the snowstorm. The local search and rescue team had left, and the other volunteer searchers had either gone to motels in Whistler or bunked up for the night at the camp. They planned to gather early the next morning to continue the search, but neither Terry nor I were willing to wait that long.

So, we decided to form a small rescue party of our own and drove to the area where Bachan was last seen. Terry paired up with his brother Ted, and I paired up with Terry's son Rick, who offered to join us. For safety, each team member was connected to the other with one end of a rope while the other end was tied to the bumper of Terry's truck. We each carried a flashlight, but our lights were quickly swallowed by the intense darkness and swirling snowflakes. It was really cold, and I couldn't see beyond my outstretched arm. We called and called, but our voices were muffled by the sounds of branches snapping and the howling of the wind. It was spooky, and the power of nature was overwhelming!

By around 2:30 a.m. we were all feeling tired and desperate. Bachan's life was on the line though, and we had to do whatever it took to find her and get her to safety.

Then, I had an idea. One of the main goals of ancient martial artists was to learn how to align their three main energy centres, or "Dantian" as they are referred to in Traditional Chinese Medicine, which would allow them to connect with their physical and spiritual powers. This concept interested me greatly, and I had spent many hours over the years studying and experimenting with chi, uncovering enough bits and pieces to learn how to align my three energy centres: one just below the belly button called the hara, one in the centre of the chest called the heart chakra, and one between the eyebrows called the third eye. I found that by lining up these energy centres, a line of communication could be established with the spirit world. As I thought about how to find Bachan, I realized I could use this method to try to gain information about her whereabouts.

However, connecting with the spiritual realm in the comfort and safety of my own surroundings was a far cry from what I would be attempting here! I had never been called upon to perform under these conditions before. Would it even work? Yet somehow, probably due to the desperate situation, I *knew* that this is what needed to be done.

So, with all this force swirling around and engulfing me, I told Rick I wanted to try something and then went deep inside myself to the calm and stillness within. Lining up my three energy centres, I asked my spirit guides for assistance in connecting with Bachan's spirit guides, and also for information regarding her safety.

Then, it happened.

Magnetic movement caused my body to sway back and forth like a stalk of bamboo in the breeze. A loving, intelligent force harnessed the energy within me, using my body as a vehicle for expression. This energy continued through to my right hand, which held the flashlight. My right arm raised up, and my elbow began bending and straightening. My hand continually thrust out with the flashlight in a pointing motion. And then, rather than subsiding, the energy flow kept getting stronger.

Telepathic communication, perhaps between my spirit guides and Bachan's spirit guides, came through as an intuitive feeling that Bachan was still alive. This gave me hope.

Rick noticed my movements and yelled out something like "What's happening?" Still swaying, with my arm whipping back and forth, I yelled back, "I'm not sure, but I think Bachan is over there, in the direction that I'm pointing!" The energy flow was quite strong, making it a bit difficult to speak.

Rick knew the area well. He informed me there was a steep cliff in the direction I was pointing, and it would be impossible to go any further. I then pulled back and gathered my energy, thanking my spirit guides.

We met back at the truck. After we told Terry what had just transpired, I proposed a rough plan of action. Terry would drive us in a circle around the area where Bachan was last seen, stopping at random points along the way. I would get out of the truck at these stops and attempt to make contact in order to further pinpoint Bachan's location. They agreed on this course of action, so off we went.

At our first stop, I got out and stood away from the truck. I once again lined up my three energy centres and called upon my spirit guides. This time, the response was instantaneous—and powerful! I could feel myself being lifted off the ground, and I heard Terry and Rick swearing and yelling in amazement. My body was continually being made to bend backwards to the maximum, then whip forward, causing my arms and hands to fling outward in pointing motions. The flow of energy was amazing, and I knew that the spirits were causing my body to point in the same direction that I had indicated previously.

We continued to make a few more stops where I repeated the same process. Each time, my body would point like a compass toward the same direction. The energy and my body movements became stronger as we went along, and I also grew more and more confident and assured of Bachan's safety. I was never hurt or scared; rather, I felt protected, and I fully trusted the intention of this strangely familiar and loving intelligence.

After we completed our circular route, we held a quick meeting. It was now about four o'clock in the morning. Terry asked if I knew what all this meant, and if I thought his mother was indeed in the direction that we had pinpointed—and most importantly, if she was still alive. I told Terry that I trusted my spirit guides. Although this whole event seemed unbelievable, I stated that I *knew* his mother was alive and well and could be found at the exact location I was pointing to all night. Terry said he felt relieved by my words and suggested we rest back at camp, then tell the search and rescue team the location as soon as they arrived in the morning.

We had a couple of hours to wait before morning light, so once we returned to the camp, I retreated undercover and meditated, thanking my spirit guides. I pondered briefly how best to approach the search team as they probably wouldn't react well to any "psychic nonsense." Eventually, I decided that I would find the right words when the moment came.

When the search and rescue team arrived, Terry introduced me to the coordinator. I simply told him that I had a hunch where Bachan could be found. After looking me in the eyes for a moment, he replied, "Hunches are good!" I walked over and pointed out a specific quadrant on his map with a push pin. He told me that they had already searched this area the day before and found nothing, but I insisted that we search it again. He reluctantly agreed. I then asked that Terry, Ted, Rick, and I be included in the search, to which he also agreed.

We jumped into trucks and headed out, a team leader guiding us to the spot where we would search. I was tired but hopeful. Once we arrived at the designated quadrant, we all climbed out of the trucks and started trekking through the bush, everyone calling out for Bachan. Although the weather had calmed down and the visibility was good, we still had the challenge of climbing over and under fallen trees and making our way across swamps and mucky terrain. Every so often, a branch would come crashing down.

After some time, I couldn't help but feel that we were not where we should be. Just as I called out to the team leader that perhaps we were not in the right area, her mobile phone rang. She then told us we were to hike back to the trucks and head out to the next quadrant, where Bachan had been sighted. I was elated but confused. Had I been wrong? Well, apparently the coordinator sent us to a different quadrant for some reason and sent two other searchers with a dog out to the actual area I had pointed out. As these searchers were calling her name, Bachan saw them and waved them down.

When we finally reached Bachan, we all wept with relief and happiness. She appeared tired, cold, and wet, but there were no visible signs of injury. A helicopter flew her to the hospital in Squamish to get checked out while the rest of us hiked back out.

On the way back, I split away from the others and hiked to the spot where I left my car (and my dry clothes).

So, there I was, standing stark naked just inside my open car door, putting on dry clothing with tears of relief rolling down my smiling face. And then IT appeared in front of me. Hovering silently just above the snowy ground was an *almost* visible bubble. It looked like a gigantic floating balloon, only without the balloon skin—and as far as I could guess, it was at least as tall as a skyscraper.

My soul instantly recognized this being as a manifestation of Universal Love. Although I have had interactions with smaller bubbles before, I had never encountered an entity of this magnitude. Its presence filled me with a feeling of loving protection, and I felt myself being embraced.

We began our communication—telepathically, in complete silence. "You don't care what we call you, do you?" I asked. "God/Allah/Yahweh/Divine?"

"NO," it responded.

"It's just a human need to identify with names and labels, isn't it?"

"YES. I AM LIFE."

"Life?"

"YES. SHARE THIS WITH OTHERS. THIS IS FOR YOU TO DO."

"You've accompanied me many times before, haven't you?

"YES."

The only way I can describe what transpired next is that IT filled me with thought and feeling packages, such as *"NO SEPARATION—WE ARE ALL ONE."*

The next section of our conversation remains fuzzy to this day, but I trust there are reasons for my current lack of recall. Perhaps I am not spiritually ready for this information yet. I do, however, recall the ending of our communication.

"NO DOUBT!"

These words reverberated lovingly throughout my entire being. I felt amazing energy in these two words, and I responded, "I promise I'll *never* doubt again." Then, IT disappeared. I don't know why I received this communication, but how could life possibly get any better?!

A short while later, Terry drove down to pick me up in his truck, and we drove back up to the camp where everyone was celebrating. I remember hearing familiar

Automatic drawing by author.

voices yelling out as we drove into camp, "Hey Jerry! We heard how you found Bachan. It was your martial arts, wasn't it?"

I'm not sure exactly how I replied, but I do recall thinking that they were missing the point. Why the focus on me and my martial arts? Shouldn't they all be looking at the big picture? Shouldn't they be wondering what mysterious force was guiding us last night—and if there is such a force, wouldn't this knowledge make them question the whole foundation of their belief system? Doesn't this prove the existence of a force greater than us, or at least prompt questions in that direction?

Everyone involved in the search gathered for lunch at a local restaurant. That's when I first became aware of a general tenseness in the air. Although a couple of people asked a few vague questions regarding the circumstances leading up to finding Bachan, everyone else basically ignored me. It's not that they were unfriendly or hostile, but there was an uneasiness in the air, and they wouldn't make eye contact. However, I could feel them constantly checking me out when they thought I wasn't looking. I also detected the faint scent of fear.

After lunch, some of us drove to Squamish General Hospital to check on Bachan's condition. It seemed to take all afternoon, but eventually we were told that aside from being a bit hungry and tired, Bachan was in surprisingly good condition and would be able to go home. What an amazing Halloween day!

Terry drove Bachan back to their home in Richmond, and I met them there to help unload supplies. It was late afternoon by now, so after we unloaded, I headed home.

I pulled into my driveway and saw my kids standing on the front porch. We waved and yelled "Hi" to each other, and as I was parking the car, my older daughter said they heard that I had been the one to find Bachan. Then she said, "Hey Dad, your chi is really strong, right?"

I noticed something in the way she said this, though I couldn't quite pinpoint what. "Uhm, I guess so. What do you mean?"

"No, I mean, we joke about your chi, but your chi really is strong, right Dad?" This time I noticed that she looked strained and her voice was shaky.

I walked into the house, and my wife (whom I've since separated from) told me that my sister Judy and her four-and-a-half-year-old daughter Bailey were dead—Judy had drowned both of them in the waters of the Vancouver Yacht Club the day before. They were pulled out of the water at 10:30 p.m., just as I passed through on my way to search for Bachan. That's why I had felt so emotional in that moment.

My sister Judy was three years older than me, and she was a caring and protective big sister. She loved all animals, rescuing and giving a home to many stray cats. She also volunteered at various care facilities for the elderly. She visited these homes regularly, taking the time to assist the residents with their lunch and listen to their stories. She never really fit into society's standards, but she spent her life forging ahead with determination and living by her own set of rules.

Judy had been experiencing mental health issues and had sought the help of professional psychiatrists. However, these sessions did little to ease her suffering—and in the end, she took not only her own life but the life of her daughter as well. The shockwaves of this event are still shaking my family to this day.

My experience on the mountain, as well as the untimely deaths of my sister and niece, changed me—or rather, it shocked me into becoming closer to the real me. I went from a state of total elation after finding Bachan to one of confusion and grief. Was there a connection between the events around Bachan going missing and the deaths of Judy and Bailey? Why, after my promising communication with the divine entity, were my sister and niece taken from life? It just didn't make sense. So, I dumped all my existing paradigms out on the floor, and only after deep pondering did I consciously put back into myself those that I believed were the truth. I wanted only the truth in life, and I had no patience for falseness.

10

LESSONS FROM THE MOUNTAIN

How do I decipher all that happened on the mountain? I realize that I cannot presume to be able to decipher all that happened that day accurately or fully; I can only interpret my experience from the level of my existing spiritual development, and share this with you.

We Are ALL ONE

I believe the bubble represents the Divine Spirit, and that all the information it communicated to me was given in truth and in the spirit of love. It's also my belief that there is only one intelligent energy in this world, and that is the energy some would call God (Source). As creations of God, we humans are gifted with the freedom to create our life experiences based on our own individual beliefs. Throughout our time on Earth, God energy is present in ALL things—humans, oceans, mountains, forests, birds, fish, even our thoughts—and we are all connected through this God force. So, in essence, God is life itself, and life is God manifested on this physical plane.

We all interpret God in different terms and names, falsely separating ourselves from those who think and believe differently. I believe that words and names are unimportant to God, and that we should grow beyond this need to be right and have others be wrong.

Many people believe that Jesus died on the cross to absolve us of our sins. However, my belief is that Jesus came to Earth to demonstrate the powers we are *all* born with, and to encourage us to strive toward attaining Christ consciousness. Rather than passing the buck by looking outside of ourselves to be saved from our sins, we must each take ownership of our responsibility and account for our own actions and thoughts.

We are all physical manifestations of God (Source), and we are all connected by divine energy. We are all cells in the same body, connected and interdependent on each other. In our bodies, the liver has a different function from the pancreas, and the kidneys have a different function from the bladder, but together, all these different parts function as a whole. One part cannot act without having some effect on the others.

Likewise, we humans are not separate from each other—we are connected by divine energy as one. When one person consciously raises his/her spiritual frequency, it raises the spiritual frequency of all others on Earth.

About a week after Bachan was found, one of her relatives held their annual gingerbread competition at their home. I wasn't planning to go as I was grieving the loss of my sister and niece, but when I heard that Bachan wanted to speak with me, I changed my mind and attended. When we met, she thanked me profusely and told me that she had felt my spirit calling for her. She sensed that we were connected by an invisible, powerful, loving energy which revealed itself to her through communication between our higher selves. and it gave her confidence that she would be found. She asked me how our connection that night was possible, but I couldn't give her an answer. All I could say is that I don't doubt that Source is *constantly* present, even though we are, for the most part, oblivious to this open line of communication.

After some time had passed since this event on the mountain, I learned that a few people who witnessed us finding Bachan—those who personally had experience with the situation—denied that anything out of the ordinary ever happened. I assume this is because admitting what happened would call for a change in their belief system, and humans tend to fear change of this nature.

Still, I was baffled. Didn't they believe that what they experienced or heard was real? Did they deny it ever happened because it's not part of their current belief system (or society's current belief system)? Perhaps because they couldn't find a believable reason for what happened, they couldn't comprehend it.

My experiences on the mountain furthered my spiritual journey, but the same did not happen for the people around me. I can only hope that they will one day be ready to receive the truth, and that their own spiritual path will then reveal itself to them.

Automatic drawing by author.

11

MARTIAL ARTS FOR THE DISABLED

I deeply grieved the loss of my sister and niece for quite some time. Then one day, while I was scribbling down my thoughts, I realized that I was experiencing this grief because I love them so much. Love is a "good" emotion—therefore, if it is accompanied by a "good" action, it will produce loving energy which can be dedicated to the dear departed souls.

So, I began offering self-defence classes for women and children in memory of Judy and Bailey. The fee to attend these classes was a donation of non-perishable food items for the local food bank and/or pet supplies for a local animal shelter. I believe that the positive energy from these fundraisers was communicated forward as messages of love to Judy and Bailey's souls.

Along with these self-defence classes, I began offering martial-arts-based exercises for the disabled. And in these classes, I saw some incredible examples of the power of chi.

Mary – Jump-Starting Her Chi

One of my students was a young woman named Mary, who had been struck on the head by a passing truck and was left a quadriplegic. She had spent years languishing in a hospital bed and was severely overweight. I visited her long-term care facility to offer classes, and when I asked if anyone wanted to learn martial arts, she instantly stuck a finger from her right hand in the air to indicate "yes!"

Mary could only move her head and right hand, so she was a challenge to teach. Fortunately, she was willing to give it her all. I began by teaching her the proper way to belly breathe as well as starting her on exercises for her right wrist and hand. Mary was a star student and practised religiously. She soon began to lose weight and became inspired to write poetry again, using her right hand to type.

One day, I noticed that Mary's muscles would involuntarily contract whenever she sneezed, causing her arms and legs to react in jerky spasms. Although I was told by her doctors that she would never regain the ability to voluntarily move her limbs, her sneezing gave me an idea.

I mustered universal energy (chi) and guided the energy through Mary, starting from her head and moving down through her body and out the bottom of her feet, literally jump-starting her personal chi. My volunteer students and I then placed an empty tin can in front of her right foot and told her to kick her foot out. To our delight and amazement, Mary kicked out with her right foot, knocking the tin can over! Needless to say, she was beside herself with joy.

We repeated this exercise every practice session. I would gather chi and guide it through her body, jump-starting her like a battery. Eventually, Mary was able to kick and knock over the tin can even when my volunteer students filled it with stones. Once her body was animated with chi, Mary also became able to voluntarily punch with her right arm. Charged up mentally and freshly inspired to work hard on her daily training, Mary lost a substantial amount of weight and regained her zest for life.

This was the beginning of our customized martial arts program.

I was anxious to share the amazing news regarding Mary's progress utilizing Chi Kung during the next meeting at Mary's long-term care facility. But when I related the news of Mary's progress to her care team (which included facility managers, Mary's doctor, and a pharmacist), I was met with a wall of denial and skepticism. They aggressively shut me down, stating that she was a quadriplegic and all her movements were totally involuntary. Despite their negative reaction, we continued our training by harnessing the healing nature of chi, and Mary continued to thrive.

Mary is an example of the healing power of chi and the positive effects which can be achieved when the subject is open to receiving them. I feel that more research should be done in this area.

Billy – Living in the Moment

Mary wasn't the only one to volunteer for this program. When I asked who would be interested in learning martial arts, there was also a man named Billy who instantly raised his hand in the air, excitedly shouting "Me! Me! Me!"

Billy's unique personality shone from day one. Highly social and outgoing in nature, he slid into our training sessions without skipping a beat. With his upbeat temperament and natural curiosity, he injected a certain liveliness and social vibe into our classes.

Prior to entering the long-term care facility, Billy had worked as a night shift foreman at a large warehouse. One day, the morning crew found him lying unconscious and bleeding on the concrete floor. He had bruising along the entire length of his body, but there was no indication as to whether he sustained these injuries by falling from a ladder or being hit by a forklift. After many surgeries, Billy was left disabled, with diminished brain function and the use of his right side only. He couldn't walk, so he was confined to a wheelchair and admitted to a care facility. Apparently, Billy's personality shifted after his accident, and he developed a childlike sense of optimism and playfulness.

To my surprise, Billy excitedly told me during our second session that we were related. He rattled off names of many of our family members, including the names of my parents—it turned out that he was married to my second cousin on my father's side. What a huge coincidence our meeting was, as I had picked this particular care facility at random.

Billy and I became close, and I looked forward to our training sessions. He occasionally called me "Sensei Jerry" (the Japanese Karate word for teacher), but he usually called me "Sifu" (the Chinese Kung Fu word for teacher) as he was Chinese and had once studied Kung Fu. He was an eager and athletic student, making full use of his good right side to punch, kick, and block. He would occasionally "surprise" me from his wheelchair with a sneak attack, which gave him great joy. He often came to class appearing listless and tired, so I would run my hands over his energy field to smooth out his body's energy flow. This appeared to make a difference; he would perk up and his body's stiff left side would loosen.

After some time of stretching and exercising Billy's left side, subsidized by the odd energy healing session, his tight body muscles relaxed and gained strength. He seemed to benefit from these sessions not only physically but emotionally as well. Billy is another example of the positive impacts that are possible when the subject is willing and open to them.

One day after practice, Billy expressed his gratitude for having me as his martial arts instructor. I replied that it was I who was grateful for having *him* as *my* teacher. I told him that he taught me more about life than I could ever hope to teach him. He taught me by displaying the true Warrior spirit in himself—his ability to be in the moment, the confidence and trust he held in his own way of being, his never-give-up attitude, his love of life, and his complete generosity toward his friends and loved ones.

I have benefited greatly from knowing Billy. I learned much more from observing him than I could ever have foreseen, and for that I am grateful.

Part 3

ENERGY HEALING AND ENERGY FLOW

Automatic drawing by author.

12

ENERGY HEALING

For many years now, I've been providing energy healing sessions. These are intuitive sessions where I ask Divine Source to allow me to facilitate loving universal healing energy. Once I establish an energetic connection to Source, I actively take in my patient's blocked or compromised personal energy field, raise the frequency of their chi, and then send this healthy energy back to my patient through my heart chakra.

I had been interested in the subject of energy healing for years, but I began providing healing sessions after one of my martial arts students suddenly experienced a back spasm during a class and pleaded for me to give him some relief. At that point in my life, I had been meditating for a few years, had experimented with healing energy on my own, and had studied acupressure and Chi Kung, but I hadn't taken any courses on energy healing. Intuitively, I held my hands over my student's back and consciously emitted healing energy through my palms. He exclaimed that he could feel something moving up and down his spine, and after a few minutes, he was pain-free. This was the beginning of my journey into intuitive energy healing.

In the early stages of my healing practice, I lacked confidence that I could actually be of service in this capacity. Once I waived all doubt, though, stronger energy healings became possible.

I feel humbled and privileged in my healer's role, especially since this is an opportunity to learn more about my inner self. By treating others, I actually treat myself and experience Spirit at work. During healing sessions, I could feel divine healing energy coming through my heart chakra, which is connected to our souls at a very deep level. The energy healing experience places me in direct communion with the Divine Source, and this connection fosters inner calm and peace. While in this state of unconditional love, it is natural to do only acts of love.

The Universe loves to heal....and heals to love

Energy healing is a method of transmitting healing energy to a patient's body through the healer's hands. The bodies of all living beings are made of energy fields, and when they are blocked or out of balance, the body/mind connection is disrupted. This leads to anxiety, depression, and a multitude of other diseases. Energy healing supports the body's natural healing abilities by moving and balancing the flow of chi, removing any energy blockages, and allowing chi and blood to circulate through the body more efficiently.

As always, we can see examples of this concept at work by examining the natural world. One example is when branches and other debris gather and form a dam in a river, creating a situation where the flow of water is impeded or obstructed. By clearing the blockage, the river returns to its normal, healthy flow.

Energy healers may use hands-on or hands-off methods of healing, or even distance healing where the healer and patient are in different physical locations. I personally employ all three methods. While there are many schools of energy healing, I rely solely on my intuition and my connection to Divine Source for guidance.

We can learn to access the healing power of chi through diligent study and practise. One exercise I teach my beginner students is to stand with feet shoulder-width apart, knees slightly bent, and shoulders lowered in a relaxed position. Place both hands shoulder-width apart at mid-torso height in front of your body, palms facing palm, and breathe normally for a few minutes while visualizing your hands holding a bubble of energy. Now clap your palms together forcefully and, with fingers pulled back, rub them briskly together until you feel heat in your palms. Exhale while keeping your hands together, palm touching palm, then while inhaling and looking at your hands, *very* slowly bring them about six to eight inches apart and hold that position. Do you notice the feeling of magnetism in your palms? Slowly and mindfully, move your hands apart and back together a few inches at a time, as if you're playing an accordion. The magnetism you feel is your chi, and your palms, in the context of Chi Kung healing, are gateways for energy that can be used to amplify and balance another person's chi.

I am grateful for the opportunity to provide energy healing to humans and animals alike. Along the way, I've experienced many situations which have challenged my existing beliefs and humbled me. I believe that my experiences as an energy healer have allowed me to "walk my bliss" and express my love honestly. On my way home after each and every healing session, I thank the Divine Source for the opportunity to fulfill my mission in life. I encourage others who are interested in this practice to become energy healers and fulfill their mission in life as well.

13

EXAMPLES OF ENERGY HEALING

I am sharing the following stories of energy healing to illustrate the power of chi. I hope these examples will help open you to the subject of energy healing and to the possibilities of your own healing powers.

Robert – An Established Paradigm

A few decades ago, I took a course in acupressure. One of my fellow students was Robert, a dentist who was interested in learning about the practice. However, due to his Western training, he was highly skeptical of the existence of chi.

Another student was a middle-aged woman named Karen, a keen student who took great interest in this subject. Unfortunately, Robert and Karen didn't get along. They antagonized each other during class and picked at each other constantly. This buildup of negative energy culminated when we all went for lunch together on the final day of the course. An argument erupted between the two, and Karen unleashed all her negative feelings onto Robert.

Automatic drawing by author.

When we went back to our classroom, Robert was noticeably distraught and wasn't acting like his usual jovial self. Class resumed, with the students pairing up to practise on each other. That's when Robert began to complain about a strange pain in his mid-torso. The pain grew stronger and stronger until he begged us to help him. The instructor, who knew I was familiar with energy and Chi Kung, asked me to handle the situation as he felt I was best suited to help. I stepped forward to where Robert was lying and held my open hands above his torso, feeling for the energy blockage. Once I located the blockage, I asked Robert if he could feel the blockage moving. He said it felt like a stick of chalk moving through his lower torso and down to his legs. I continued guiding the blocked energy down his right leg and out the sole of his foot, and then I dumped the negative energy into a nearby wall. Robert was elated, calling me the Chi Master, and declared his newfound belief in the existence of chi.

About a year later, Robert and I bumped into each other at a coffee shop in Vancouver. After exchanging greetings, I asked him how he felt after the traumatic event in class. He looked at me questioningly, saying he felt fine. I reminded him of our experience on the last day of the acupressure course, but he just looked at me blankly, then denied anything unusual had happened. Could this meeting with Robert serve as yet another example of someone "forgetting" an experience because it was too much of a challenge to his current belief paradigm?

I'm aware that some readers might be questioning whose version is correct at this point. I understand that this story could raise skepticism and doubt in your minds, but it is my hope you will be open to the possibility that my story is true and gain some benefit from all aspects of this experience.

Samuel – A Science-Based Answer

Another time, my friend and student Maia introduced me to her cousin Samuel in hopes that I could send him healing energy. Samuel had been sickly since he was a child, to the point that he carried a bag of medicine around with him at all times. He was living in the USA and working as a scientist at a research university.

Samuel, although somewhat skeptical, was willing to receive energy healing from me. We set up our long-distance healing sessions via email, and all healing sessions were scheduled for his bedtime so he could then lie in bed comfortably and receive healing energy.

These sessions worked out well for him. In short time, he began to notice improvements in his health, such as his eyesight getting stronger. His doctor charted these improvements and began reducing his medications, and eventually, Samuel's health improved to the point where he felt relatively healthy overall.

Coming from a science background, Samuel wondered what exactly caused his dramatically improved health. So, he flew to Vancouver, where I met with him and Maia. He thanked me for all the sessions I had done and asked me to explain in scientific terms what it was that had caused his healing. I responded that I had no scientific answers to his question, but he was adamant that I give him one. He had previously asked one of the senior scientists at his university what he understood about energy and healing, but he could only offer up the term "dark energy" as a possible explanation. Samuel told me that he couldn't believe in any of his healing unless he was given a science-based answer that he could accept.

Although I still do not have answers for him, the response of the senior scientist leads me to believe that quantum physicists have begun to uncover much on this topic. Perhaps we will soon have an answer to Samuel's questions.

Kyle – Sticking with the System

Kyle was one of my young adult martial arts students who was diagnosed with stage four brain cancer. Although his mother was very skeptical of energy healing sessions, she contacted me because Kyle knew of my involvement with healing energy and hoped that I could help him somehow. I met him at their home and began our first session. My body moved with unusual intensity in this session, drawing out his sick, turbid energy and dumping it through the floor into a receptive Mother Earth.

During energy healing sessions, I enter into a deeply meditative state and consciously connect with Divine Source. In one of the sessions, while I was in this altered state, Kyle's left arm began involuntarily moving. It reached toward his brain and seemingly grabbed handfuls of sick energy, then tossed this wad of energy in my direction. I would "catch" this sick energy and punch it down through the floor and into the ground. After the session, Kyle asked how it was that he was able to use his left arm—he had previously suffered a stroke, which paralyzed the entire left side of his body. I could only assume that this was Universal Love at work!

These healing sessions were going well, and Kyle was feeling much stronger. But one day, his mother abruptly cancelled our scheduled session and admitted him back into the hospital. I met up with her in the hospital lobby, where she explained to me that although my sessions with Kyle had drastically improved his health, she simply couldn't accept the concept of energy healing. Even if Kyle would likely die in the hospital, she would at least have the comfort of knowing that he was part of a system she knew and believed in. Although saddened by her decision, I empathized with her and understood how she felt the need to go with what she believed was her only option.

Steve – The Power of the Written Word

One person I was fortunate to know was Steve, a kind and sensitive middle-aged man with tremendous grit and courage. He had been battling stage four cancer for five years when I met him and had originally been given only months to live. However, Steve was unwavering in his belief that he would regain full health through practising Chi Kung every day, maintaining a positive outlook on life, faithfully taking herbal medicine prescribed by his holistic doctor, and receiving energy healing sessions. He acknowledged to himself each morning that he was living in a healthy, vibrant body, and he continued to enjoy good health for many years. I would drive to his house to provide energy healing sessions on a regular basis, and we became close friends in the process.

Life was going in a positive direction for Steve until friction arose between his two sons. One of the sons felt that Steve had taken the side of his brother, and he began continually calling him or dropping in uninvited to complain. All this discord caused Steve a significant amount of stress, but that didn't stop his son from harassing him.

It finally got to the point where Steve felt the need to compose a letter to his son, pleading him to stop. He wrote that he was dying from cancer and the stress of his two sons fighting was too much for him to bear.

Shortly thereafter, Steve's health deteriorated to the point where he was bedridden for much of the day. When Steve showed me a copy of his letter, I suggested that his deterioration in health might have been related to his conceding that he was dying of cancer—by writing the words, he had affirmed it in his mind. I suggested that Steve try to make peace with his son, but the continued rift between the two brothers made this impossible. The sparkle in Steve's eyes faded, and he sadly passed away.

I think that once Steve wrote that he was dying and read his words written in ink, he instilled in himself the belief that he was indeed dying, becoming a contributing factor in his demise. This is a sad example of just how powerful our beliefs are.

Jimmy – Mother and Child Bond

One day, my friend Ellen called me in desperation; her seven-month-old son Jimmy had suddenly stopped accepting her breastmilk. The doctors had been running various tests on the baby but couldn't come up with a reason for his mysterious behaviour, and they obviously couldn't ask Jimmy as he was too young to talk.

Ellen knew that I can communicate telepathically with animals, so she wondered if I could communicate with her young son as well. I had no previous experience in communicating with human babies, but Ellen asked if I would try. Of course, I couldn't refuse, and we met at her home.

When I opened and connected to Jimmy's energy, his response was immediate. Jimmy indicated that he was healthy, with nothing physically stopping him from drinking his mother's breastmilk. Instead, he told me that the issue was with his mother and directed me to shift my focus to Ellen.

After a brief discussion with Ellen, we found that the rapidly shifting dynamics of their usually stable home environment was at the heart of the problem. First of all, Ellen's husband Ron was heading to work in Northern BC for six months, leaving Ellen alone to take care of Jimmy and his two siblings, both of whom were under the age of six. Ron's parents were also leaving on an extended holiday, so Ellen would not have their usual support.

The intimate bond between mother and infant allows them to share in each other's energy fields. It appeared that Jimmy was picking up on Ellen's feelings of loneliness and anxiety and was responding to them by refusing to drink. This in turn caused Ellen to blame herself for being an inadequate mother, which increased her anxiety and tainted the energy of her breastmilk even more. It was a vicious cycle.

After talking it over, Ellen and I decided that this might be an opportune time for Jimmy to start on formula—the emotional stress of Ellen's current position would not be easily resolved, so she didn't consider working on her sour breastmilk issue a viable approach. It's been a few years since our session, and to this day both mother and son are doing well.

Through this experience, I learned that human babies use energy as their foundational way of communicating. This means we can communicate with them telepathically, so long as we learn how to connect to those energies.

Calligraphy by author, titled "Maternal love."

14

WHERE ATTENTION GOES, ENERGY FLOWS

One year, my friend and former student Dan asked me to teach at one of his summer hockey camps. One particular group of young men who were participating in my martial-arts-inspired dry-land training program—seven gifted and focused hockey players between the ages of eighteen and twenty—felt that they could benefit from additional sessions. So, we set up a series of early morning workouts specifically for them.

I enjoyed these extra classes immensely. Their natural curiosity, honest work ethic, and group spirit inspired me, and I envisioned how they each had the potential to become true leaders in their communities.

With this thought in mind, I approached them one morning with the statement that they were much more than the sum of their hockey skills, and that both in and out of the rink, they should be aware of making conscious choices to create their future reality. They all acknowledged that in their hockey training, they were pushed to be aggressive—to think that they must fight to prove their toughness, and that intimidation is the only way to realize their goals.

I suggested to them that they were capable of rising above this aggressive mindset and displaying *true* leadership and courage by balancing their priorities in life. I then mentioned that it's relatively easy to hurt (or kill) someone, and that there are consequences for their choice of actions.

I also explained that for every yin, there is a yang. So, if we are able to physically practise and research techniques for killing, then we must be able to heal by using those same methods with different intentions. For example, Dim Mak, the art of striking specific points on your opponent's body to critically injure or kill them, is physically very similar to Chi Kung, which is practised for the purpose of health, spirituality, and mastery of the martial arts. It is the intention behind these two approaches that make the difference in how they affect others.

Finally, I explained that if we can build and regulate the flow of chi either inside or outside our bodies, our organs will be in a state of balance. If our organs are balanced, then we will become healthier and stronger. And if we can work toward becoming physically healthy and mentally disciplined—if we can feel that oneness with the cosmos so often spoken about—then we can balance that "dark" side of ourselves (aggressiveness to the point of hurting others) with the "light" side (healing energy).

I also suggested that we can affect the energy of others from a distance, without ever touching them. We can choose to either injure internal organs or become a conduit for healing energy, and we make this choice through conscious thought or intention.

This last point caught their attention. They didn't think it was possible to affect someone from a distance and asked me to demonstrate on one of them—and being young, testosterone-filled men, they particularly wanted me to demonstrate Dim Mak. *Oops*, I thought to myself. *I just put my foot in my big mouth.* I declined to demonstrate, explaining that affecting the chi of others was not to be taken lightly or treated as a parlour trick.

Well, this went over like a lead balloon—my feeble excuse just added fuel to the fire. After all, in their minds they were young, strong, and invincible. How could anything hurt them, especially from a distance? Not giving in, they kept pressing me to show them what I meant. Eventually, I realized that I couldn't expect any of them to accept such incredible claims without any sort of proof. It was time to put my money where my mouth was while remaining aware of my responsibility to keep them safe from harm.

I reluctantly asked, "Okay, who wants to volunteer?" They made a group decision that Trey would be suitable as my subject for this demonstration. Trey was in great shape, had a calm and focused mind, and had proven himself to be a tough competitor time and again. It was a good choice.

When Trey stepped out of the group, I placed him on a spot a few feet in front of me and asked the others to back away from our immediate area. I then reminded them of this very important point: that intention (conscious thought) controls emitted energy (chi). As intention plays a crucial role in achieving the desired results, I would have to suppress my intention, which would therefore suppress my emitted energy, to avoid harming Trey. I hoped that the use of my body movements alone would be sufficient to illustrate the concept of how one might heal or balance someone's personal energy, and then how one might go about disrupting or unbalancing it.

Standing a few feet in front of Trey, I began by going through the motions of the healing and balancing process. To those observing, these movements would appear as though I were waving my hands toward my intended subject. While I was doing this, I gave a running commentary on the interaction of energies being emitted by me and received by Trey.

Next, I demonstrated how I would disrupt or unbalance his personal energy. These particular movements would appear more aggressive than the first set. I made sure to suppress my emitted energy to avoid harming Trey—this demonstration was only meant to give a hypothetical example of what might happen if I deliberately focused my energy in this way.

The so-called demonstration ended with everyone milling around quietly. Although they smiled weakly out of politeness, their disappointment was obvious and the lesson seemed to miss the mark. I knew what they were thinking: after such incredible claims, shouldn't the demonstration be more spectacular? There were no lightning bolts shooting out of my hands, no "aha!" moment, just an airy-fairy non-lesson.

I called the disappointed group together to quickly go over their thoughts on this before resuming our workout. We had barely begun when Trey muttered something so quiet it was barely audible. We continued talking, but then Trey interrupted. "Actually, I'm a bit woozy."

We all stared at him in silence; he looked ill. "Actually, I don't feel good." He started to wobble and lose his balance, so I quickly ran to hold him up. You could have heard a pin drop in that room! I helped him over to the side of the room so he could rest. He tried to sit on the footing of an exercise machine, but he fell off. By now, the others were falling to the floor themselves, hooting and hollering and slapping at each other. I helped Trey up and walked him to a bench on the other side of the room. I told him to sit still, and to rejoin the group once he regained his balance. I also apologized to him.

All the others surrounded me, laughing and giggling. Of course, they wanted to know what happened to Trey. They all witnessed that we were a fair distance apart, so I obviously never physically touched him. How could that be? This was all so surreal to them. I told them we would discuss it later, but for now we would continue our workout.

Soon Trey felt better and rejoined the group, trying his best to work out again. I felt bad for him, so I stood behind him, mustered up universal healing energy, and emitted that energy toward him.

The group began firing questions at me at the end of the session, but time ran out and they had to run off to complete the rest of their day's training.

Feel much more than physical Touch – be at ONE!!

Later that same day, I stood in the gym waiting to teach my scheduled afternoon session. My early morning group also took part in this class, so I was anxious to hear how their day's training went. Soon they ran excitedly into the room shouting that they wanted me to affect them with energy the way I did with Trey. When I refused, they offered to sign waivers releasing me of all responsibility. They just wanted to feel what Trey felt! Of course, I refused again, only offering my apologies.

Then Trey came running in, beaming, and exclaimed to the group that this had been his best day of training yet. He told everybody he had noticed that I had emitted energy toward him after his balance was affected earlier in the day. He also noticed that his energy level and skating performance had been much better than usual, lasting throughout most of the day.

Now they all wanted answers as to how I was able to affect Trey—and more importantly than that, they were now more engaged in the concept that we are able to affect other people's energy.

I explained to them that although my intention and emitted energy were suppressed during the morning demonstration, some energy must have inadvertently escaped through my eyes, which were open and focused on Trey. Where attention goes (even unintentional attention), energy flows! I then explained that because I was feeling badly for affecting Trey so negatively, I had used my power of intention to smooth and balance his body's energy flow.

Although I was glad Trey felt so healthy and charged for the remainder of the day, I also felt remorseful. My responsibility as their teacher was to keep these people safe from harm, and yet I had allowed them to coerce me into a demonstration that had inadvertently affected one of my students. Even though it turned out well for Trey, it was a sharp reminder to myself that attention is key, and that energy manipulation is never to be taken lightly.

Automatic drawing by author.

89

Part 4

ANIMAL COMMUNICATION

Drawing channeled by a canine patient.

15

WINGS TO FLY

I don't recall when I first became aware of my ability to communicate with other species, but for many years now I have been able to open my heart to the energies of the animals around me and speak with them telepathically. I'm humbled that these animals trust my heart enough to speak with me in this way.

Unfortunately, not many people are able to forge such a connection with these creatures. In fact, humans tend to mistreat animals—it's imbedded in our way of life, and many are okay with it. This might be due to our mistaken belief that, outside of our pets, animals have no feelings, no family bonds, and no soul.

In the instances when I've been fortunate enough to communicate with animals, they have shown and requested love, not hate. In the few instances where they have displayed seemingly bad or negative behaviour, I have learned that they were displaying natural, instinctual responses to their situation. We humans tend to view their behaviour through distorted lenses as we already have a preconceived outlook of all animals, viewing them as being lesser than us. They are *different*, and humans don't tolerate differences very well. Our intolerance to differences (even between humans) creates a separation between us. And by creating this false separation, we lose sight that all of us, animals included, are living beings created by ONE source.

Hopefully, we humans will soon wake from our drunken state and clue into the truth that we have no more right to this earthly plane than any other species. And we are making movements in this direction—for example, in January 1990, Pope John Paul II proclaimed that animals have souls.

Automatic drawing by author.

I am grateful to all animals for the teachings they have given me over the years. They live in the moment of NOW and are not bothered by regrets of the past or fears of the future. At times, they have surprised me with their wisdom and challenged my existing paradigms.

A few decades ago, I felt the need to communicate with the animal kingdom at large. I had previously been successful in contacting the oversouls of the whales and elephants, so I chose them to represent all animals. Once contact was established, I asked, "How may I be of service to you, the animal kingdom?"

They answered, "*Help us tear down the invisible false walls which humans have created. These false walls separate humans from each other as well as from all other living beings. They create narrow, confining corridors which restrict the way you walk your human journeys.*" This sound, loving, and wise advice from the animal kingdom is certainly worth pondering.

If you are interested in learning how to communicate with your pet, there are websites and books available on the subject. However, I would suggest that a good place to start is meditation. If you are not into traditional meditating, you can just sit quietly in loose, comfortable clothing with a straight back (but not too rigid—allow your lower back to relax softly) on a comfortable chair, eyes closed. Cup your hands on your lap, one on top of the other, both palms facing the sky. Take a few minutes to just sit while breathing naturally—if you are familiar with belly breathing, all the better. Then, place your tongue to the roof of your mouth* and become aware of your breathing. Pay attention to your inhales and exhales. Visualize your breathing as waves flowing to and from the shore, and then break your breathing cycle into four parts: inhale (wave incoming), slight pause, exhale (wave outgoing), slight pause. Continue this breathing cycle for as long as you feel comfortable. By mindfully keeping the rhythm of your breath constant, you'll notice that your body becomes more relaxed with every exhalation.

After you have become accustomed to this breathing exercise, I suggest that you spend some time breathing while focusing on your heart chakra—the spot at the centre of your chest, halfway between your nipples. This will train you to drop into your heart and open to others, including your pet.

In addition to using this breathing exercise during meditation, I also recommend making it a habit in your daily life. Becoming more mindful of your breathing will open a doorway to improving your health, cultivating inner stillness, and connecting more deeply to your own spiritual powers. It will also reduce stress and increase your calmness and focus, one breath at a time.

At the core of successful animal communication is the combining of both words and pictures. When you send a question to your pet, you may also accompany it with a mental picture which correlates to what you are saying, thinking, and feeling. Allow all messages you receive back to occur naturally, even if they don't make sense at the time—don't try to force your pet to communicate in a way you'll understand. Eventually, you'll learn to interpret these messages with more clarity.

When you're ready to attempt to communicate with your pet, find a moment when they are lying down or otherwise in a calm state. With eyes closed, ask Divine Source to connect you to your pet (using their given name as well as your surname to avoid contacting someone else's pet). Place your attention on your heart, then visualize your pet and send an invisible string of love to them. Now place your attention on the space between your eyebrows; this is your third eye and is the gateway to your spiritual powers of communication. With eyes still closed, "look" through your third eye and focus attention on your pet. Using your third eye as your mouth, silently call your pet's name: "Hello, is this [pet's name and your surname]?" Then, ask if you have permission to speak with them. Wait a moment, then ask a simple "yes" or "no" question (such as "Are you happy?" or "Are you hungry?") and be aware of any subtle response. Try not to expect immediate results. Have patience, and repeat this exercise as often as you want. Hopefully, one day, you'll make a connection.

You can also try this on wildlife or on farm animals, but most of these animals don't have given names. So, you can instead choose one of the animals, focus on it, and call it by the species. Good luck!

* Note: The reason you need to place your tongue to the roof of your mouth during the breathing exercise is because energy continually runs through and around your body in channels (like a train runs on train tracks). The main energy channel in our bodies runs from our tongue down the front of our body to our perineum, then from the perineum up our spine, over our head, and down to the roof of our mouth. When your tongue touches the roof of your mouth, it creates a connection, also called an "energy bridge," which makes for a strong flow of energy in your body.

When we talk or otherwise have our tongues away from the roof of our mouths, we create a gap in the flow of energy. The energy will still jump across the mouth and continue its flow, but the flow is weakened. It's like turning off a light switch, which creates a gap in the flow of electricity.

16

KOKORO

Throughout my pre-teen and early teenage years, my main hobby was raising pigeons. At one point I kept between twenty and thirty birds; I loved every one of them and had a name for each one. I scavenged around the laneways in my neighbourhood, finding old lumber and receiving donations of hardware (nails, door handles, screws, hinges, and more) from friendly neighbours. From these scraps I built a walk-in bird cage that had its own screened-in flight pen. I kept records of each bird's ancestry, lineage, and health in a journal and knew their individual personalities. After school, when my mother would release the birds to fly free, they searched for me and picked me out from my friends, landing on my arms, shoulders, and head. I felt great enjoyment in watching them fly and perform their amazing acrobatics, and I would spend as much time as possible just sitting and being with them in the coop as they went about their lives.

I would often ride my bike to visit Bob, an experienced pigeon fancier who specialized in raising champion rollers. These are pigeons that are bred for their unique ability to fly to a high altitude, then free-fall toward the ground while rolling in successive backward somersaults, pulling up at the last moment and beginning their climb back into the sky. Rollers are often entered in competitions to see which bird can complete the highest number of successive rolls in one go.

During one of my many visits, Bob told me that one pair of his champion flyers were neglecting to sit on their egg, and he gave it to me. I rushed home with this tiny treasure and placed it under one of my nesting pigeons. Like an expectant parent, I hovered over the nest and kept constant vigil. When the time came for the pigeon to hatch out of his shell, it took a huge effort on his part. The shell was unusually hard, but he didn't give up—he was determined to see this world.

I helped him break through the last part of his shell, and I think he imprinted on me and saw me as his parent. He was a runt, much smaller than the other birds, but he was handsome! He was a beautiful golden colour with a compact, solidly built frame. He also possessed an inner spark—a spiritual quality which I hadn't noticed in the others. He would often seek me out to sit on my shoulder or outstretched arm, and we would simply hang out together. Because of his calm yet confident demeanour, he soon became my favourite.

Whenever I released my birds out of the pigeon coop for their daily exercise, they would flap around momentarily to get their bearings, then quickly gather into a close-knit group and begin flying in circles above the coop. They would fly higher and higher into the sky until the majority reached their comfort zone, and then they would stay at that level. A few of the rollers would continue to climb so they could perform their acrobatics, but soon they too would find and stay at their level of comfort.

But even after all the other rollers stopped climbing, my golden bird would keep up his spiralling ascent into the sky. He didn't accept the limitations set by the others. I would stand and watch with pride as his small body became a tiny speck. Then, there would be a slight pause when time stood still—when his wings stopped flapping and he was suspended in air. He would stretch back with his open wings as his tiny head arched backward. This was his "point of power"—that magical moment when he surrendered to his trust and became free. Rolling in rapid backward somersaults, he would hurtle toward the earth in an amazing free-fall display. His golden feathers would become a spinning pinwheel reflecting the sunlight; it was beautiful to watch. At the last possible moment, he would pull out of his free-fall and climb back upwards to the sky.

What was that inner quality he possessed which made him so special? *His belief in himself!* He didn't accept the limiting beliefs of the others, trusting his own inner map instead.

My golden pigeon brings to mind the Japanese word *kokoro*. Here in the West, we may translate kokoro to mean heart. However, in Japan, many do not consider emotion and intellect as being separate, so kokoro translates as a mixture of heart, mind, and soul. When used in the martial arts world to describe a person's character, this word takes on a much deeper meaning; it is generally reserved as a complimentary expression to acknowledge an individual's exceptional spiritual strength and purity. Kokoro was the word Kaicho Seikichi Toguchi used to give me the confidence to start my own branch of our Karate school.

This little golden pigeon stands out in my memory as one who displayed the rare qualities of spiritual strength and purity, along with a total belief in his own inner map, each and every time he took to the skies.

Automatic drawing by author.

Fly Homeward!

During these years, I invested hours upon hours into interacting with my pigeons. Often, I would just sit silently and observe. They trusted me and were very accepting of my presence—but as a slight downside, I can identify with those stone statues covered with pigeon droppings!

Eventually, I began to uncover interesting parallels between pigeons and humans. For instance, when it came time for the young birds to try their wings, I noticed that there was always a special moment when each of them realized that they were born to fly. With a leap of faith, they pushed off from their safe perches and launched into the unknown. Some must have doubted themselves after the fact, judging by the wild flapping, but eventually each of their wings found air.

Much of their early stages of flight were spent experimenting and discovering (or uncovering) their inborn abilities. With time and perseverance came the confidence to fly higher and farther, testing their limits—or in some cases, their limitlessness.

There are many breeds of pigeons, each unique in their own way. One is homing pigeons, which are known to be extremely strong flyers, born with the ability to find their way home from distant and unfamiliar release sites. The best ones didn't need to fly with the flock, trusting only in their individual intuition to make their way home.

There are conflicting theories about how homing pigeons are able to navigate incredible distances and find their way back home with such apparent ease. I believe they rely heavily on their ability to sense the earth's magnetic field—invisible energy lines which run in, or slightly above, the earth's surface—and to utilize these magnetic fields as a map to help guide them on their individual journeys. However it works, one thing is for certain: pigeons are born fully equipped for their life journey. They know what they are, and they live their lives accordingly. We humans can learn much from them!

I believe that as humans, we are born into this world as spiritual beings inhabiting a physical human body with the purpose of gaining experiential lessons. The moment we become aware that we each have a higher self, our metaphorical wings unfold and help to lift us above the bondage, chaos, and limitations of this physical realm.

Some of us, though not many, uncover (or discover) our wings and leave the nest, but most prefer to stay with their two feet planted firmly in the ground. To me, "leaving the nest" might refer to the conscious intention of cutting any chains holding you to the preconceived notions of others and working honestly to become that which you, as an individual, really are—to take wing and find your way.

Automatic drawing by author.

As with the homing pigeon, continued focused awareness and conscious effort bring about a knowing deep inside, and you can begin to tap into the invisible, intelligent source of energy that guides you along your individual journey to becoming your higher self. Trust in the love and support from unseen guides, which act as strong currents of support for your wings. Trust in your wings to always fly you homeward as you COME to BE your true higher self.

OPEN WINGS – BECOME WINGED OPERATOR IN PERSON OF SPIRIT...

17

SCOUT AND REX

On Sept 2, 2003, I received a phone call from my friends Joe and Pam, informing me that their beloved German shepherd Scout had passed away after a lengthy battle with cancer. In previous communication sessions, Scout echoed what so many other dying pets have said to their humans:

"Don't waste energy by wondering whether you made the right decisions for me in the past or worrying how much longer I'll stay with you on this earthly plane. Cherish this moment we have together. Look at me, be with me NOW and feel the love that exists between us."

This is a lesson we can all learn from. There is only today, and there is no holier moment than NOW!

Joe and Pam asked if I would communicate with Scout's housemate Rex (a shepherd/collie mix) from my home to find out if he was okay. They also asked if I would try to communicate with Scout's spirit to see if she was okay as well.

Shortly after we finished our phone conversation, I attempted communication with Rex. Contact was immediate. Rex was grieving—he made the back of my hands beat against my forehead repeatedly, and I could hear him wailing in despair. I apologized

Drawing by author.

for interrupting his grieving, told him I would close our contact for now, and asked if I could contact him later. He replied "yes," so I left him to grieve. I later found out from Joe and Pam that at the time of our communication, Rex was frantically trying to dig up Scout's body.

A short while later, I attempted a communication session with Scout's spirit. At the time, my dog KT was lying down on the living room floor while I was sitting on the couch a fair distance away. At the moment of contact with Scout's spirit, KT validated our communication by whining sharply. She then scrambled up to me and, sitting with her head in my lap, looked up toward Scout's spirit. KT had been with me numerous times while I meditated, practised Chi Kung, and performed distant energy healing. She was used to watching me gyrate and wave my arms, and she'd never reacted this way before. Scout messaged me that she knew this was her designated time to cross over into the higher realms, and that she was at peace.

That evening, I drove to Joe and Pam's house. We sat around the dining room table, with Rex lying on the floor about six or seven feet to the left of me. Once again, I began communicating with Scout's spirit. I asked if she had a message for Joe and Pam, and Scout communicated her love for them. I then asked if she could send Joe and Pam a message through me to somewhat ease their grief.

Scout then showed her image to me. In this image, she looked in my direction, then walked (or rather, glided) up a short flight of stairs to a door which was partially open. She walked into the room, pushing the door open a bit more, and then laid down on the floor, looking at me.

Asking her to show me more, Scout once again showed me an image of herself. This time, she walked into what looked to be a cabin. It had no porch or front steps, and there was a small pile of chopped wood sitting on the dirt to the right of the doorway. After asking her to continue, she sent me a visual of blue sky and tall trees, then homed in on an image of a tall rock with a slightly rounded top. Behind the boulder stood a tall pine tree. For some reason, we zoomed in for a close-up of the branches at the upper part of the tree.

I then asked Scout if she had anything to communicate to her companion Rex. As she answered "yes," her upper torso became increasingly visible to me, and I intuitively opened my energy bubble to include Rex in our energy connection. Rex validated our three-way communication by suddenly rising from the floor and quickly walking over to me. He sat with his chest pressed against my left thigh, his eyes fixated in Scout's direction.

Joe ordered Rex to back off and apologized to me. Remaining focused so as not to lose contact, I told Joe that it was okay—that this was Rex's moment with Scout. Scout then sent "bullets" of energy (perhaps thought packages or feelings) to Rex. These bullets, followed by visible trails of colour, travelled in clusters toward Rex's head. It felt like I was a facilitator connecting Scout's spirit with Rex. It was an amazing event!

I thanked Scout, and we agreed to connect again soon. I then disconnected our communication and delivered Scout's messages to the best of my ability.

Joe and Pam were able to provide some context for the first image. They lived in a two-storey home, with their bedroom located up a short flight of stairs, and they leave their door partially open every night so that the dogs and cats can move about. I believe Scout was telling them that she would still come to visit and guard them at night while they slept. Interestingly, Joe and Pam found Scout's favourite toy just inside their bedroom door the following morning, even though she rarely brought this toy upstairs and Rex never played with it. Perhaps she left her toy as a sign to Joe and Pam that she was still with them.

The second set of images baffled everyone. Joe asked if Scout could have shown me a tool shed rather than a cabin as he had a pile of chopped wood stacked against his shed. However, his woodpile was situated in a different spot from the woodpile Scout had shown, so I still had a strong feeling that Scout had shown me a cabin. And while Joe and Pam did go hiking with the dogs quite a bit, they couldn't remember a tall boulder with a rounded top or the tree behind it. I suggested that they keep these images in their minds over the next few days.

Three days later, I received an email from Joe and Pam telling me that they went to one of Scout's favourite hiking spots: Cabin Lake at Cypress Mountain. So, *this* was the "cabin" Scout had shown me! She wasn't pointing to an actual, physical cabin; she was referring to the location of Cabin Lake. Joe and Pam had found the tall boulder in front of the pine tree, and while Joe was carving Scout's name in the boulder, they

A raven in the tree at Cabin Lake.

The tree behind a tall boulder.

Carving Scout's name onto the boulder.

noticed a raven sitting in the spot Scout had indicated. I found the presence of the raven interesting as it resembled Scout's appearance but in bird form.

Then, on September 7, I felt Scout's spirit calling me. So, I opened myself up and connected with her spirit. Contact was immediate and unusually strong, which surprised me somewhat. I can't remember exactly what questions I asked, but she made me tap my third eye area repeatedly while what appeared to be an image of her upper torso formed out of bits of energy.

Next, a raven's image formed from the same bits of energy and blended with her form. This combined form then took flight. It was a beautiful, blissful, unconditional spiritual love connection!

Scout also used both my hands and gestured from heaven, through my body, and down toward the earth in a sweeping circular motion. At the time, I felt she was conveying a message regarding the cycle of birth to death and back to birth again.

I felt a strong urge to produce this piece of artwork—to bring into the physical realm the image Scout sent me after she passed away. I felt that this fairly accurate representation of Scout's visual message was meant as a parting message for Joe and Pam.

It was as though Scout was whispering to me, and I was once again being in service as her vehicle for this communication.

This particular piece of artwork held a different vibe for me than usual. I was focused and couldn't stay away from it, but I also felt a certain amount of detachment from it. I was simply recording a private visual message without imparting my own style or conveying any particular concept. Joe and Pam now have the artwork hanging up on their living room wall.

As with the many layers of colour and paper in this artwork, every so-called coincidental event in our lives contains multiple levels. It is up to us to decide whether or not to peel away at each layer and ponder its teachings.

Cut paper art by author, titled "Scout and the Raven."

18

THE INTUITION OF HORSES

I don't have much knowledge of horses as they have never been a part of my life, but I have always admired their beauty and power. And through my communication sessions, I have found that horses have a unique gift of being able to sense and heal the cracks in human energy fields.

Chester – Macho but Sensitive

My friend Janice is an avid horsewoman and an animal lover. At one time she underwent medical treatments for a serious health issue, but soon she was back riding her horse, Chester. However, she was still in recovery mode and, being physically weak, had lost all confidence in her strength and in her ability to ride him safely. She also could detect a difference in Chester's attitude toward her, so she asked me to communicate with him at the stables to figure out what was going on.

I started by introducing myself to Chester and asking him for his permission to connect energetically. I then asked him to scan his body and give me a reading of his

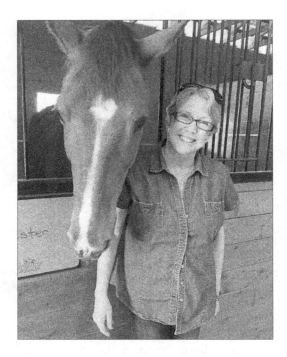

Chester and Janice.

overall health status. Whenever I ask an animal to scan their bodies, my own physical body moves involuntarily, like a mime, following their focused attention.

We began scanning his body, starting from his head and face and working our way down. All seemed fine until the moment we reached his back end. I found myself hunched over at the waist, with my head lowered down toward the ground and my eyes staring up at my groin. I could sense that Chester was in a frustrated and questioning state of mind. I am not familiar with horses, so this confused me. Janice giggled, then told me she found it comical because Chester had been castrated and was now a gelding—obviously, he didn't like it!

In spite of this, Chester proudly thought of himself as a powerful, healthy, athletic stallion, and he felt hindered whenever Janice rode him. When I related his feelings to Janice, she became quite sad, knowing that she was holding him back and wasn't being a full partner to him.

After a few more communication sessions with Chester, it became clear to Janice that her beloved horse was unhappy and required a more active, unrestrained life. Janice ultimately made the agonizing and unselfish decision to re-home Chester to a riding ranch on Vancouver Island where he would be cared for and would get plenty

Chester greeting Janice.

Sharing a precious moment.

of opportunities to run and jump with able, experienced riders. Chester is now living to his full potential, and Janice travels to visit him as often as possible. To this day, they continue their strong bond with each other.

Chester was a powerful, macho horse, but he also had a sensitive side. One day, Janice brought Tianna, a troubled high school student whom she had taken under her wing, to the stable to visit with Chester. Tianna immediately felt at ease with Chester and spent the entire afternoon hanging out with him.

When I arrived later that afternoon for a scheduled communication session with Chester, he was eager to establish contact and to channel a personal message to Tianna. Apparently, he had picked up on Tianna's personal emotional issues. He told her that he was well aware of her personal chaos, but he could clearly see the divine spark in her. He suggested she follow a career working alongside horses, and that she would eventually uncover her special gifts which she could present to the world. This message seemed to have a dramatic effect on Tianna—she hadn't been aware that Chester was "reading" her and listening to her thoughts the whole afternoon. I do not know if Tianna followed Chester's advice, but I hope she was able to uncover the special gift he saw in her.

Horses have a unique ability to read our auras, and they try to heal our energy fields. For this reason, horses are now becoming used for mainstream therapy, and horse therapy stables have become available to the general public.

Trapper – Intuitive

Trapper is a young stallion who, at the time that I met him, had been recently purchased by his new owner, Tara, a young woman in her mid-thirties. My friend Janice, who wanted things to go well between Trapper and Tara, asked me to communicate with Trapper and introduce them to each other in order to break the ice.

When I arrived at the stable, it was obvious that Trapper had much to say. As soon as we began our session, Trapper warned that an older female in Tara's family had serious health issues, and that she should see a doctor. Tara—who was a skeptic of animal communication—denied all of this at first. However, after a bit of questioning from me, she hesitatingly told me that her elderly grandmother was indeed quite sick, but she was in denial and refused to see her doctor. Tara was confused and wondered how Trapper knew about her grandmother.

Automatic drawing by author.

Note: Author believes that the "baby" being held in the automatic drawing refers to the birthing of a new humanity.

Trapper then made a strange request, asking Tara to bring her filly to visit him. Tara was flabbergasted! She started crying and told me that she was going for her third and final attempt at getting pregnant via in vitro fertilization. Given Trapper's message, I suggested that she would be successful in her attempt—and in fact, Tara had a healthy baby girl later that year.

How was Trapper able to come up with such accurate information? I don't have any science-based answers, but I do know that energy is the language of animals, and we all share in this intelligent energy. Perhaps Trapper picked up this personal information from Tara's energy field.

19

TAWNY AND MAMIE

Tawny was a gorgeous older Rottweiler, and I was called by her owner to communicate with her and to do an energy healing session. Tawny had been diagnosed with advanced cancer, and her veterinarian had said that nothing further could be done for her through conventional Western methods.

Just as I made contact with Tawny and began to question how she was feeling, she interrupted me with a visual of a fragile, thin, heart-shaped piece of glass coloured in hues of red, green, and blue, with a yellow streak running down its centre. This visual was obviously very important to her as she repeatedly showed it to me. Her owner, Cora, couldn't figure out what the meaning was, nor could I.

The following day, we got our answer. Cora's ex-husband, who helped raise Tawny and was very close to her, had experienced a heart attack that night. He eventually recovered, which was good news. However, it's interesting how Tawny picked up on this and felt it was more important to communicate a warning of his failing heart than the state of her own health.

When I communicated with Tawny in our following session, I asked her how she felt about leaving this physical plane. She responded that she was ready to move into the higher realms and asked Cora to spend quality time with her in order to truly see her love rather than concerning herself with how much longer Tawny would be here.

In my experience with animals, I have found that they aren't afraid to cross over—to them, it's a natural transition. They aren't concerned with how long they've lived, or how much longer they'll have on this earthly plane. Instead, they're concerned about their humans being in the moment—the moment of NOW.

During one session, when Tawny was feeling particularly tired, she raised herself off the floor to face me. She walked up and put her head between my legs, harnessing my body to send her weakened energy up and through to my mouth. After receiving my permission to use my voice, Tawny's message came through me as spoken words meant for Cora's young-adult daughter, who was struggling with personal life issues at the time. Concerned for her safety, she advised her to "stick close to Mom" and to "listen to her advice."

Tawny lived with her housemate, a young labradoodle named Mamie, who had a wild and crazy personality. She was unruly and lacked discipline, but she was extremely lovable. She was very possessive of her small blanket and would carry this blanky around the house, hiding it in her crate so that she could lie on it at night.

Cora asked me to communicate to Mamie about Tawny's failing health, just to see how she would react. So, I shared with Mamie that Tawny was sick and would soon cross over. After she received this news, Mamie stood still for a moment, as if pondering the situation. Suddenly, she bolted out of the living room, ran down the hallway, and skidded into the bedroom where she slept. We all wondered what she was up to, and our answer came when she appeared back in the room, carrying her precious blanky in her mouth. She walked up to Tawny and placed her blanky on the floor in front of her, then took a few steps backwards and sat down, staring at her blanky. In a demonstration of compassion, Mamie had presented her most cherished possession to her dying housemate! This gesture touched us deeply and serves as a reminder of the love that resides in the hearts of animals.

As her time for crossing over got closer, Tawny asked me to assist her shift into the higher realms, and of course I agreed. In our following sessions, I raised the frequencies of both her energy and my own to help smooth Tawny's transition to the higher realms.

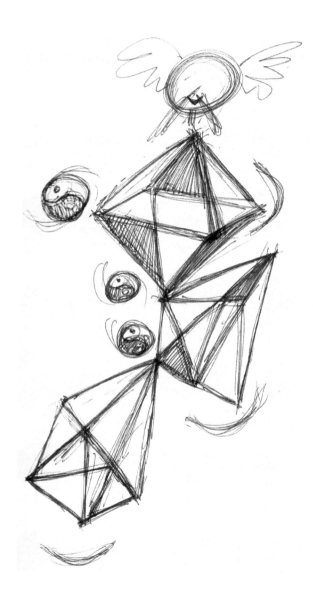

Automatic drawing by author.

20

UNCONDITIONAL LOVE

I met Beau, a male Brittany, in January 2007 when he was already a senior. His human companions, Bob and Bev, had adopted him about four years earlier from a shelter in the USA. His life up to that point had been one of abuse and neglect, and he had more than a few issues to address, but the unconditional love and care he received from Bob and Bev worked wonders on him.

Shortly before we met, Beau had stopped eating and was just lying on the floor, with no energy. He was x-rayed by a local vet clinic in Surrey and diagnosed with arthritis and advanced cancer. They recommended chemo treatments, but Bev balked at the idea.

Knowing that Bev preferred alternative ways of healing, they suggested she see my friend Dr. D, a brilliant veterinarian who served her animal clients through holistic and alternative methods as well as Western ones. Dr. D started Beau on a regime of Chinese herbs and suggested Bev and Bob contact me regarding energy healing and animal communication sessions.

Beau responded immediately to my energy healing work and made fast progress. He got back on his feet and began eating with enthusiasm. He was able to resume his outings at the dog park and was once again willing and able to go for daily walks.

To confirm the positive health results from my energy healing sessions, Bev ordered two more ultrasounds two months apart from a vet clinic that specialized in cancer. The specialist was surprised at the results of Beau's second ultrasound, which showed remarkable remission. The doctor told Bev, "I don't know what you're doing, but keep it up." However, when Bev told him that I was providing energy healing sessions, it didn't go over very well.

After Beau's third and final ultrasound, the specialist became defensive, saying that perhaps they were wrong with their original cancer diagnosis. However, Bev had possession of the initial ultrasound which clearly showed Beau's cancer, so she knew he was in denial due to his skepticism of energy healing.

Not everyone denied what was happening, though. One of the veterinary technicians followed Bev out to the parking lot to ask her what treatments she was doing. After Bev told her about the energy healing, the technician strongly suggested we continue them.

I did more energy healing sessions with Beau, and he continued to enjoy a healthy life for some time. Then, one day, he communicated to me that his time to transition to the higher realms had finally come—his health was starting to deteriorate, and the cancer had returned. He asked me to assist him in his transition to the other side, and I agreed.

Coincidentally, at this time Bev had decided to go for her master's degree. I informed him of her plans to enrol in university, and Beau, knowing the closeness of their relationship, realized that he couldn't cross over yet. His passing would devastate Bev and impact her ability to study.

So, I began energy healing sessions with Beau once again. Always sensitive to his beloved Bev, he would tell me when he had received enough healing energy and ask me to instead channel clean, healthy energy to her. He would faithfully stay by her side while she studied, supporting her with his personal energy and his heart.

It took some time, but finally the day arrived when Bev earned her degree. To celebrate, she arranged to meet one of her classmates for a celebratory dinner. But while she was at dinner, her husband Bob called her. He and Beau had been at the Langley dog park when Beau fell into a hole in the ground, breaking his leg. Bob had rushed him to an emergency vet clinic for x-rays, and they found that the cancer had pushed his organs closer together and made his bones soft. Since Beau was fourteen years old, they decided to end his suffering and put him to rest.

Beau had been ready to leave this earthly plane two years prior to his passing, but he hung on until Bev achieved her goal. People generally say "I would die for you" to express their love, but Beau said "I will live for you."

Most of us are aware that we share a strong bond with our pets. However, many of us are unaware that this close bond creates a sharing of energy fields that is visible to our pets but invisible to us humans. The language of animals is energy, so it's natural for them to "read" our energy field, which contains information on our health and emotional state.

I'm often asked to communicate and possibly do an energy healing session with a sick or dying pet. On numerous occasions, the pet will communicate and receive healing energy, and once their needs are addressed, they will direct my attention to their human. This usually comes as a complete surprise to the human, and some will even become defensive, adamant that there is nothing wrong. In most cases, the pet is correct, and is revealing hidden emotional issues or health concerns in an effort to seek healing for their human.

Automatic drawing by author.

Forever Love

A couple of months after Beau's passing, I was called to do another communication and energy healing session on Woody, Bob and Bev's latest furry family member. I had communicated with Woody several times before to help him with some breathing issues, and I had learned that as a young dog, he had been trapped in water under a thick sheet of ice and nearly drowned—that was the reason he would have episodes of panicked breathing.

During this particular session, I was communicating with Woody when some of Bob and Bev's dogs who had passed on (including Beau) came through as a group in spirit form. They came to assist me with Woody's healing, and to relay a message.

I was in a standing position next to Woody with my feet shoulder-width apart when I felt their energies flowing through my body. My personal energy was rooted into the ground while both my arms and upper torso were guided to move in concert, forming an infinity symbol in the air. I also visualized individual sparks appearing in front of my eyes, the sparks representing each of the individual souls present. They whispered the words "forever love" in my ears before disappearing into thin air. They were sending a message that they were here in spirit form to support Woody. They wanted to be recognized as being the energy of unconditional love, and as being in the "forever" realm.

As a self-study project, I sculpted the image of my experience with wire and melted solder and titled the piece "Forever Love." The bottom of the image depicts being rooted into the ground, the main body of the image forms the shape of a heart, the top portion of the image illustrates the infinity shape that my arms and torso traced in the air, and the individual spots of solder indicate the individual spirits that came forward. I very much appreciate these loving spirits for coming through with this message.

Wire and solder sculpture by author, titled "Forever Love."

21

ANIMALS AS NATURAL HEALERS

My friend Flora loves and respects all animals. She has a special affinity for them, and they respond to her in kind.

Flora shared her home with two pet tortoises that she rescued when they were babies. One was a male named Linus, and the other was a one-eyed female named Mydas. One morning, I received a call from Flora. She had taken Mydas to a vet clinic because she couldn't move her head very well, and she had a lump on her neck. Flora asked if I would perform a long-distance communication with Mydas to see what the problem was and if there was anything I could do to help her.

When I got off the phone, I connected with Mydas. When I connect with an animal, I usually take on the animal's energy field, wearing it like a bodysuit. I essentially "become" the animal. I asked Mydas where the problem was, and she used my right arm (like a flipper) to point at the lower left side of my neck where the neck and shoulder meet. Just to make sure, I asked her to point out the problem spot again, only this time using her left flipper. She used my left arm to point at the same spot at the lower left side of my neck.

She agreed to partner with me to direct healing energy to the problem area, so we proceeded to do a long-distance energy session. Once this part of the session was finished, I asked if there was any other problem area that required attention. She said there was, then guided my hands to extend straight out in front of my body and move in short, vertical brushing movements. It was as if she was floating in the space directly in front of me, and my hands were making caressing movements up and down her tiny frame. When we were done, she thanked me and I disconnected from her energy field.

Later in the afternoon, Flora called to give me feedback on Mydas. It turned out that the reason Mydas couldn't move her head was because she had developed a neck infection, which led to an abscess under her skin. The vet informed her that the abscess had somehow hardened into a little marble that popped out onto the table as soon as she cut a small opening in the skin. Mydas could now move her neck freely.

This made sense, but I was still wondering why she guided me to do the vertical brushing movements. I questioned Flora about it, and she too was bewildered. But then, about an hour or so later, Flora called me from home. She was excited to share with me the reason why Mydas required those movements: she had just laid an egg!

Mydas with her egg.

Now it all made sense! Mydas had wanted help with her body's energy flow to assist in her egg laying.

During this phone conversation, a thought struck me about a possible reason behind why Mydas had developed her neck infection. I questioned Flora about it, and she confirmed that she herself had been suffering from chronic pain in that same spot for the past year. I believe that Mydas mirrored Flora's health symptoms in order to protect her, consciously taking on the sick energy to reduce the negative impact on Flora's health at a cost to her own well-being.

Petra – Sharing energy fields.

This is not the only time I saw one of Flora's pets take on some of her sick energy. Flora also had a pet bunny named Petra, with whom she was very close. About one year after Mydas' egg incident, Flora was suffering from chronic bladder issues, and eventually Petra developed similar bladder symptoms as well.

This protective behaviour is based on unconditional love, and I have been fortunate to witness it in many pets. I wonder how often pets are diagnosed with a disease due to them protecting their owner the best way they know. I also wonder how many humans recognize this act of love.

22

BRING HEAVEN TO EARTH

Karma was a cat who was in a state of perpetual filthiness. She could very well have been named Pig Pen after the messy character from "Peanuts," but I named her Karma instead because I somehow knew she had much to teach me.

We met in March of 2002 while I was building a pigeon coop for the SARA Society, a non-profit animal rescue organization in Surrey, BC. While SARA is mainly devoted to saving cats, they also provide shelter to dogs, birds, and whatever else lands on their doorstep.

I found myself in their backyard, hastily taking final measurements for the flight pen of the pigeon coop and feeling overwhelmed by all the cats. In those days, I was more of a dog person. Well, to be truthful, I was actually terrified of all cats (and highly allergic to them). And now here I was, surrounded by over a hundred of these unruly bags of mush with claws attached, all wanting a piece of me!

Donna, the dedicated woman who runs the SARA Society, was busy picking up cat poop and chatting with the cats when I noticed a tiny, sickly kitten hobble over and extend her paw for attention. Donna called out, "Why, here's little Bailey!" which instantly brought to mind my young niece who had died in 1994. I asked where this

Karma

scrawny little kitten had come from and found out she had mysteriously appeared the previous day. The volunteers named her Bailey and brought her to the vet clinic to have her checked out. Sadly, Bailey was diagnosed with feline leukemia and wasn't expected to live very long.

Donna questioned my strong reaction to the name Bailey, so I told her about the drowning of my sister and niece eight years prior. I also mentioned that there was something about this young kitten which reminded me of my niece, but I couldn't put a finger on what.

I began reminiscing about Judy's passion for rescuing and caring for homeless cats when suddenly there was darkness all around us. Then, a light from above shone a spotlight on what appeared to be an old mop on the porch. On closer look, what I thought was a mop was actually a filthy, scruffy white cat. And it was a mess, with chewed ears, a protruding and bleeding eye, missing patches of fur, scabs and green pus covering the skin, and a naked tail with more twists and turns than my bathroom plumbing. It was howling in frustration as the other cats harassed it. Shocked and slightly repulsed, I asked Donna what this cat's story was.

"She's an approximately eight-year-old Persian/Himalayan mix," Donna shared, "brought in by an elderly woman who had no use for her any longer. She doesn't get along with any of the other cats, and they pick on her constantly. She won't mix with other cats—never enters the living room and stays under my bed when indoors. She needs to be fostered or adopted because she's having a nervous breakdown by being here and probably won't live much longer, but nobody wants such a messy, smelly cat."

Despite my negative impression of cats, I felt sorry for this being. So, when I got home, I asked my wife Val (who is a cat lover) if we could foster her until we found someone to adopt her. Val agreed.

We drove to the SARA Society and were invited into the living room where most of the cats were gathered. "Where's the cat?" asked Val. At that point, the cat appeared and, much to Donna's surprise, walked into the living room and brushed past my leg. She then walked straight to the front door and looked back at us as if to say, "Let's get out of here!"

Once she was in our home, she clearly felt safe as she immediately walked out of her carrier. She walked up and introduced herself to our border collie KT (who winced at her rank odour) and made herself right at home. She was like a whole new cat!

After many fruitless days of searching for her new forever home, it became obvious that nobody wanted her because she was too hard to look at and needed too much maintenance. We realized that it would be cruel to take her back to SARA, so we decided to adopt her permanently and to rename her Karma.

I drove to SARA to sign the adoption papers, and as soon as I sat down, little Bailey came into the room. She stared at me for a moment with her large, innocent eyes, then struggled up onto a chair. From there, she made it onto the table, sat down and stared at me again. I asked, "What is it, Bailey?"

She arose and slowly walked up to me, putting her nose to my nose. Then she reached up and, placing both front paws around my neck, gave me the softest, sweetest hug! Tears flooded my eyes. I believe that Bailey the kitten was connected to the spirit of my deceased niece Bailey, and that she was placed here to bring my attention to Karma, who I believe was connected to the spirit of my deceased sister Judy.

I was so emotional that I don't remember what transpired after that hug. It was all such a blur that I don't even remember signing the papers. And a day later, Donna informed us that little Bailey passed away—perhaps her job was done.

We took Karma to the vet clinic for a check up, coming home with an Elizabethan collar around her neck and an assortment of medications for her to take. After a few days, we realized that the reason she came to us in such a bad physical state was because she was stressed out, and that the collar and medications were only adding to her stress. So, we took the collar off. We told her that we loved her, that she never had to worry anymore because this was her home, and that we'd always take care of her.

Interestingly, some new fur sprouted over the next few days, and then all the missing fur gradually grew back in. The swollen and bleeding eyeball returned to a healthy state, and the scabs on her body eventually disappeared. Despite some initial hesitations, Karma and KT eventually became friendly housemates. She formed an especially close bond with Val and spent many evenings curled up on her lap.

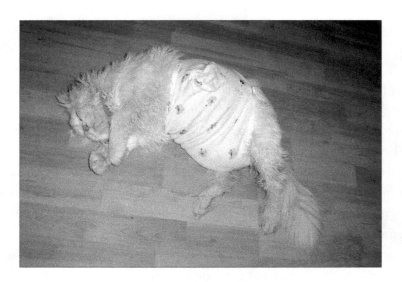

Karma – a past of abuse and neglect.

I communicated with Karma on quite a few occasions, and she gave us an overview of her personal history—one of abuse and neglect. She had birthed litters of kittens and still missed her babies.

During one particular communication session, I asked if she had any messages for me. Her instant reply was, "Please, please bring Heaven to Earth!" At the time I didn't know what she meant, although it had been a recurring message to me from my spirit guides.

Karma shared eight years with the author and his family.

In another session, I asked if she had any wishes. "Yes" she answered, and she mentally took me upwards and through to higher frequencies. We travelled further until we arrived at an island floating in space with a huge doorway on it. We flew to the doorway, where a large hand appeared and turned the doorknob, opening the door. Karma and I flew through the doorway to the vast expanse on other side. At the time, I had no idea what the door or the space behind it signified. Today, though, I take it as the "open door" of my soul which leads to the unlimited realm of potential.

The next day, while Val and I were out running errands, I mentioned that I was wondering about the meaning behind this communication session with Karma and whether it related to her message to bring Heaven to Earth. At that moment, the song "Stairway to Heaven" came on the radio. Coincidence or what?

Living with Karma changed my opinion of cats. Through the emotional content of our many telepathic conversations, she taught me that love can reside in the scruffiest of bodies, and that no human has a greater right to be here on Earth than any other species.

After being with us for eight years, Karma peacefully died in our arms, surrounded by love.

23

KT AND KIT

KT first appeared to me in a dream in 1998, in which I was shown a border collie that I was to find and adopt. She had an image of my logo on her snout, except the human figure of my logo had been turned to face a mountain to meditate. I immediately began searching for this border collie from my dream, visiting all the animal shelters in the Fraser Valley with no luck.

After a long, fruitless search, I received an unexpected call from one of my martial arts students. After mentioning my search for this border collie, she told me of her sister-in-law who just happened to have a five-month-old border collie pup which needed a new home due to changing family circumstances—and sure enough, she had an image of my logo on her snout. We fell in love with each other, and we were inseparable from the moment we met. Her name was Kate, but I called her KT—short for Kara-Te.

When I brought KT to my dojo to meet my students, she fit in perfectly! Life at the dojo stimulated her growth, and she blossomed into a beautiful, healthy one-hundred-pound dog. Over time she learned proper dojo etiquette and found her place beside me in front of the students, like a sheep dog standing beside a shepherd.

KT watched over me, not only protecting me from other dogs but also protecting

KT – author's soul mate.

my health. For example, one day I was demonstrating how to do a proper forward roll for my students. While I was mid-roll, KT let out a loud howl from the far side of the room. Instantly she was at my side, pressing against me to stop any further action on my part. She spent the following two days hovering over me, monitoring and stopping me from doing anything physical. I was annoyed at first, asking her to leave me alone, but then my right shoulder began to seize up in pain. She had somehow known that I had compromised my shoulder and was trying to prevent me from injuring it further.

KT was born lifeless and had to be resuscitated, and this affected her brain-to-body function. Our vet warned me that she would be sickly and in the vet clinic often, probably dying at an early age. Thankfully KT proved the vet wrong, going on to live a normal, healthy life.

We spent many happy years together until suddenly, at the age of twelve and a half, her health began to fail. She communicated to me that her heart was tired, and that she would leave this earthly plane when the rainy season began. Hoping to extend her life, I began doing energy healing sessions on her to keep up her strength and to improve her health, and she expressed her gratitude to me.

One afternoon, she requested a healing session. Then, during the session, she told me she was gifting me (the healer) the experience of being healed. Suddenly, my body began moving involuntarily, and I started hopping and twirling in circles. I felt the healing, and it was a wonderful once-in-a-lifetime experience!

As the end of her time on Earth approached, KT and I spent our time just being with each other. During this time, she communicated to me, *"Don't wonder if you made the right decisions for me in the past, or how much longer I will have on this earthly plane. Cherish this moment we have together. Look at me, be with me NOW, and feel the love that exists between us."*

I had relayed this message from dying pets to their human companions many times, but this was the first time I had received this valuable teaching myself. This message from KT was very personal and all the more meaningful coming from her. After that message, I became more aware of being mindful of the moment of NOW.

Then, early one morning in October, I awoke to the sounds of laboured breathing. We communicated, and KT allowed me to feel the numbness of her body so that I could know she was not experiencing any pain. Lying in my arms, she relayed messages of love for me and Val, and we reciprocated with our messages of love for her. And then I saw her spirit leave her body as she crossed over.

Later, I walked to the window and, through tear-filled eyes, looked out to find rain pelting down. The rainy season had arrived, just as she had informed me.

About a week later, I communicated with KT's spirit, questioning why she would go through all those healing sessions only to suddenly pass on. She told me that she had asked for the healing sessions so that she could gift me, one who healed others, the special experience of being healed. KT's spirit communicated that she was staying around my energy field so that I could connect with her at any given moment.

She also communicated that she was searching for a puppy. I wasn't open to having another dog in my life, so I asked her why I should need one. She answered, "To support you on your continuing spiritual journey." She informed me that we would find this puppy before Christmas, that it would be a female of mixed breeds, and that it would come from a local rescue shelter.

Soon after, Val and I met with our seven-year-old grandson and discussed possible names for our yet-to-be-found puppy. He left to "talk" with KT's spirit to see if she could give him a good name, then returned a few minutes later with the name KIT written on a piece of paper. When asked how he arrived at this name and if it had any particular meaning, he said that he was trying to contact KT when the letters K-I-T suddenly popped into his head. He thought the letters might have stood for "keep in touch." We tearfully agreed that our new puppy would be called Kit.

I later communicated with KT, asking her if she suggested the name to my grandson. She confirmed that she did, but the letters actually stood for "KT's in training" because she was now undergoing training as a healing spirit to support animals who have crossed over from neglect or abuse. She spent her entire time on this earthly plane focused solely on protecting me, and now she'd been given the opportunity to protect many, many souls.

I spent hours connected with KT's energy, searching rescue websites for puppies needing homes. I would point to a particular puppy's photo and ask her if it was the one. She would then get my hands to wave in dismissal or get me to shake my head "no." We went through many animal rescue websites, always with the answer "no."

Eventually, KT guided me to the SARA Society site, which had a blurry photo showing a litter of pups. KT pointed and made my head nod "yes!" KT then pointed to one particular puppy and made me nod again. From the photo, she looked like a real plain Jane—the type that typically gets passed over time and time again. I asked KT a few times if she was certain this was her chosen one, and each time KT confirmed her choice.

Kit – KT's chosen one.

So, we did find our new puppy before Christmas, she was indeed female of mixed breeds, and we found her at the SARA Society, the local animal rescue shelter that we had been supporting for years—coincidence or what?

This little bundle of trouble was a challenge right from the start. She was full of piss and vinegar, with a strong mind of her own. However, with consistent training and loads of love and patience from my two young grandsons, this pup grew into a loving, intelligent furry family member.

When Kit turned six months, I took her to the vet clinic to be spayed. That morning, KT's spirit visited me and whispered "passing the baton" in my ear. I didn't understand the meaning of her message, but I was confident that all would become clear in due time.

That afternoon, I picked Kit up from the vet clinic and brought her home. Once home, I rolled her over onto her back so that I could give her an energy healing session at the site of her operation, and what I saw made my hair stand on end. An image of my logo (a mirror image of KT's mark) had somehow appeared on Kit's tummy!

Peaceful Warrior logo.

KT's birthmark on snout.

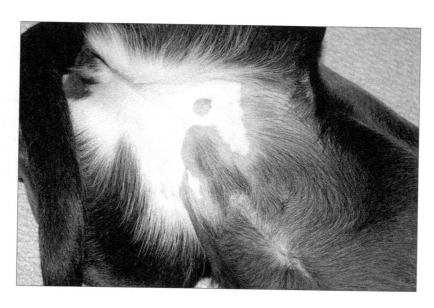

*Author's logo as it appeared on Kit's tummy
(a mirror image of KT's birthmark).*

I have no idea how KT accomplished the transferring of the image, but not everything is explainable in life. Thank you, KT!

Angel on My Shoulder

Even after her passing, KT remained close and protective. She stayed connected to my energy field, and I could call upon her at any time to communicate.

One day, I received a call from a gifted psychic and life coach named Chloe. She had heard of my animal communication sessions through our common clients, and she asked if I would come to her house to meet and communicate with her two dogs. She particularly wanted me to communicate with her chocolate Lab, Pie, who worked alongside Chloe in her practice. Pie had unusual talents and was able to sense a person's emotions; Chloe could tell how the client was responding by watching where and how Pie would position herself. However, Pie had an alpha personality and saw herself in the alpha role in their relationship. This was causing problems in their working relationship, and Chloe was looking for an answer to this issue.

Chloe also had another dog, a bearded collie named Ingo, who was submissive. Her only issue with him was that he would ignore her commands.

I drove to Chloe's home and knocked on the door. The dogs began barking, and, while Chloe answered the door, three things happened simultaneously:

1) Both barking dogs rushed toward me, with Pie in the lead.
2) I felt KT's spirit jump off my right shoulder and land between myself and the advancing Pie, which caused Pie to immediately stop in her tracks.
3) Chloe exclaimed, "Look! She jumped off your shoulder!" She had seen KT— and obviously, so did Pie!

I came in and sat on the living room couch; Pie appeared to be shell-shocked and stayed a safe distance from me (and KT). I advised Chloe to talk directly to Pie, and we would form a four-way conversation. Whenever Chloe spoke or questioned Pie, an invisible universal interpreter appeared, creating a language which Pie could understand. Pie then communicated her answers to me, and I would relay the message to Chloe. It turned out that Pie regarded Chloe not as her alpha owner, but instead as a partner/sister. So, she had decided to take on the role of boss. It took a lot of back-and-forth discussion, but eventually Pie promised to make attempts to shift their working relationship.

During our communication session, KT must have relaxed her guard as Pie began to gradually close the distance between herself and me, eventually lying calmly beside me on the couch.

As for submissive Ingo, he needed someone to lead and protect him, and he didn't obey Chloe because he didn't respect her. He didn't see her fulfilling her role as his protector. This was something Chloe would need to work on.

This experience proved to me that pets can see the spirits of the deceased. I believe that KT's spirit really did accompany and protect me on this visit. After all, she was obsessed with being my protector on this earthly plane, so why wouldn't she continue in spirit form? My desire is that this story will provide hope to those who have lost a dear pet and show that contact continues after death.

24

MINI LESSONS

I have included the following short stories as further examples of how animals have the ability to think and relay messages to us. I hope you'll find these stories thought-provoking, and that they will be of benefit to you.

Bao Bao – I'll Consider It

Sometimes people ask me why I don't just tell a pet to correct their negative behaviours. The answer is that all pets are individuals—just like humans—and they each have their own character. Just because they can understand me doesn't mean they will simply do as I say! My biggest challenge is convincing cats who pee on furniture or mark their territory to stop this behaviour. It seems that most cats feel that their actions are explainable, not negative or destructive in any way.

One day, Dr. D called me to communicate with a pampered Pekingese named Bao Bao who had not pooped in four days. After making contact with Bao Bao, I learned that his owner had recently brought home a puppy, and Bao Bao was jealous. So, this

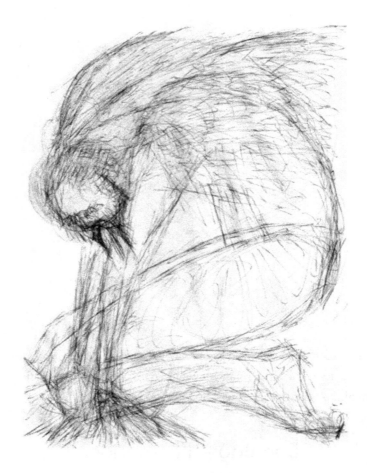

Automatic drawing by author.

was his way of protesting. I mentioned to him that his human was worried for his health and told him how dangerous what he was doing was for his system; he wasn't impressed and stood his ground. I repeatedly asked Bao Bao to please think about the harm he was causing himself and the trauma this was causing his human. He was still unimpressed. I then reminded him of how loving his human has been, that his human promised he would still be her first love, and would he please consider pooping to show his love for her? After a long pause, he then promised to "consider it."

I later learned from Dr. D that as soon as Bao Bao got home, he jumped out of the car, squatted, and pooped! So, he did seriously consider my words after all.

As with humans, our pets often won't do something they don't believe in. However, by reasoning with Bao Bao, I was able to help him understand how important it was that he should poop. It doesn't happen very often that a pet will change its mind over something it feels strongly about, but I'll take any wins I can get.

Just a Cow

Many years ago, I suggested to my wife that we become vegetarians due to the cruelty subjected upon farmed animals. However, I have food allergies that made it impossible for me to commit to becoming a true vegetarian, so I instead promised to become a pescatarian, allowing myself to consume seafood.

This dietary change went well for a while, but as time went on, my craving for meat grew stronger and stronger. I would fantasize constantly about eating fried chicken and roasted duck, but I never cheated—I reluctantly stuck to my promise for six years.

About three blocks from our house, there was a small farm with two cows and a bull. One day, still wrestling with the guilt caused by my intense desire for meat, I walked over to the field and began a conversation with one of the cows. I asked, "Hello, dear cow, may I communicate with you?"

The cow answered, *"Yes."*

"What do you think of my species eating your species?"

"It is natural, if you require our bodies for sustenance."

"You animals trust me and allow me to communicate with you. What do you think of me if I desire to eat your meat?"

"We do not judge."

"You do not judge as we humans do?"

"No."

"So, what can I do for you in return?"

"Teach humans to treat us with respect and compassion rather than mistreating us and causing us to suffer such pain."

This was one example of the awareness and wisdom found in a so-called dumb animal. Animals don't judge; only humans do!

After this communication session, I went back to consuming meat. However, I now take a moment before eating to appreciate the animal who gave up its life, I include many plant-based food options in my diet, and I have become even more involved in supporting animal welfare associations.

Automatic drawing by author.

My Whale Experience

In the year 2000, my younger daughter (who is now a veterinarian) worked in Telegraph Cove on Vancouver Island as a naturalist for the local whale watching company. Knowing of my interest in whales, she invited me aboard for one of their expeditions.

Once we were out on open water, I was guided to a spot on the boat where I would get a particularly good view of any whale sightings. Soon, my daughter spotted a pod of whales at a distance and noticed a newborn calf in the group.

We were in a normally quiet strait, which whales gravitate toward. However, word got out about this pod of whales, so many whale seekers rushed into the area. The whales found the noise and vibrations from our boats to be very disruptive, so they began to move themselves and their baby away from us. I realized what was happening, so I took the opportunity to quietly establish communication with the pod. Being careful not to be too obvious in my movements, which would disturb the other passengers, I told the whales that I loved them, congratulated them on the birth of their wonderful new calf, and asked if I could have a closer look at their baby.

Instantly, the pod turned around and began swimming in our direction. Despite all the noise from our boats, they came closer and closer. I assumed they felt my loving intentions and decided to show me their baby. As they neared our boat, I felt the deep throbs of drumming from their collective hearts pounding in my chest. And as they dove under our boat in a tightly knit group, I could hear the words "LOVE . . . LOVE . . . LOVE" echo in my ears. I could barely contain my excitement. I asked the other passengers if they heard or felt anything when the whales were under our boat, but nobody responded.

Humans tend to disregard the feelings of wildlife and take their needs for granted. In this case, the whales were protecting their calf by actively moving away from the noise and chaos of their surroundings. By changing course and swimming under our boat, they displayed their true nature of trust, acceptance, and love.

A Sensitive Soul

When I think of a dog who lived solely for her family, Skya comes to mind. I was asked by Mariah, Skya's owner, to communicate with her beloved standard poodle. She was robust, young, and healthy, so she didn't need any energy healing—Mariah was just curious about what she had to say.

I connected with her and asked how she was doing. Rather than communicate about herself, she immediately replied with anxiety and worry about her family. She showed me an image of Mariah sitting with her husband, Jack. She highlighted Jack's groin area while physically sharing her feelings of anxiety with me. I mentioned this to Mariah, and she was stunned. She then told me that Jack had just been diagnosed with a hydrocele that morning, which is water retention and swelling of the testicles. He required surgery and was quite nervous and upset about it; apparently, so was Skya.

Over the years, Skya and I had many communication sessions. She would always be waiting to communicate with me whenever she picked up on any sick energy in her family, which created much anxiety in her.

This is just one example of the sensitivity our pets have around our health and their ability to read our energy field.

Part 5

THE OTHER SIDE OF THE VEIL

Automatic drawing by author.

25

LIFE – STRANGER THAN FICTION

There have been times when life has handed me strange experiences which challenged my existing paradigms. These experiences were obviously meant to happen for a reason but are not readily explainable. They do, however, point toward the existence of life in other dimensions in their own cryptic way of being.

We live in a multi-dimensional world, but we are trying to decipher mysteries of the Universe with only our five senses. I have included these stories because I believe that we are not meant to fully understand or have all the answers to the mysteries of life. Sometimes, questions are more important to spiritual growth than answers.

Geometric Visitors

For some time, I would occasionally awaken from my sleep conscious of something (or someone) observing and studying me. I would open my eyes to the sight of a strange geometric entity either hovering over me or moving slowly toward me. These were clearly sentient beings who would instantly become aware of the fact that I had noticed them and head for a wall or travel along the ceiling in order to disappear from sight.

I started keeping a pen and a pad of paper on my bedside table so I could record what I saw. Yet I was unable to draw these entities, which were a weird meshing of various geometric shapes not of this dimension. Regardless, they seemed loving and intelligent. I wondered if they were visiting me from a higher dimension—and if so, why?

Eventually, I decided to try communicating with them telepathically. Once I connected with them, I asked if they were from/of the loving Divine Source. They responded "*YES.*" I told them that I was bewildered by their presence—that I was still in the infant stage of my spiritual development—and asked if they would send me something more basic which would be easier to grasp.

A couple of nights later, I was once again stirred from my sleep and opened my eyes. Floating in the space above my bed was another entity, but this time it didn't play shy and disappear from sight. Instead, it stayed in place, allowing me to draw it. It appeared to be made of geometric shapes from this third dimension, and I was able to easily sketch it on my pad of paper.

I sketched two red balls, one placed vertically on top of the other. I then drew what appeared to be a group of green, wiggling, worm-like creatures. Once I completed my drawing, I thanked the entity. It seemed to acknowledge me, then moved into the wall and disappeared.

The following day, I was babysitting my infant grandson and went to his dresser to find something for him to wear. As I rummaged through his drawer, I came upon a few newly bought t-shirts that I had never seen before. I took one out and unfolded it—and then my hair stood on end! On the front of this new t-shirt was the graphic of a green octopus with eight waving arms and the number eight in red ink beside it. This was the entity which I had drawn!

That was the one and only time I was visited by an entity that I was able to capture on paper. All the following visitations were once again by odd-shaped entities that I was unable to draw.

To this day, I wonder what or who these strange sentient entities were and the reason for their visitations. I don't know how the image of the entity appeared on my infant grandson's t-shirt or how they knew that I would be looking in his drawer for a t-shirt that morning. I am assuming that these entities were visiting from a higher dimension, perhaps to assist in my spiritual growth.

Automatic drawing by author.

In Dreams

I sometimes experience what I call waking dreams. These are times in which I'm aware of being in a dream state while simultaneously having one foot in my waking reality. These dreams are usually accompanied by some type of spiritual message.

One night, I dreamt of being in an old, unlit house, unable to find any working lights. Scanning the darkness, I noticed my Aunt E in the kitchen, looking forlorn and holding a knife to her right wrist while pacing back and forth.

Then, from out of the darkness, a handsome young couple entered the kitchen and asked me my reason for being in this dream. I was slightly confused by the situation and pulled out of my dream to the reality of my bed. Then, after realizing the danger my aunt was in, I made the decision to go back in and protect her.

Upon re-entering my dream, I reached out with my right hand to knock the knife away and then covered my aunt's wrist to stop the bleeding. Suddenly, the two young people transformed into grotesque figures with angry expressions, and they began ferociously attacking me. I fought them off with my left arm and leg while dragging Aunt E out of the dream scenario. Once I was back in the safe reality of my bedroom, I lay in bed with questions rolling around in my head for the rest of the night.

The following day, I called Aunt E on the phone and asked how she was doing. She replied that she was feeling depressed and wasn't doing very well. I began telling her about the dream I'd had, and when I reached the part where she was pacing back and forth in the kitchen with a knife at her wrist, she blurted out, "Oh my God, Jerry! You saved my life!"

She went on to tell me that a young couple in her apartment complex had died in a car accident, and she decided to attend their funeral. During the funeral, she started feeling weak and depressed (she has a history of bouts of deep depression), so she walked outside and sat on a bench to grab some fresh air and clear her mind. Instead, she began feeling hopelessly distraught, so she went home. There she fell into a deeper chasm of negativity, then opened a drawer and took out a knife. She began pacing the floor with the intention of committing suicide by slicing her wrist. Then she told me, "Suddenly, you came into my mind, and I put the knife down."

After I related the remainder of my waking dream to her, we tried to make sense of this intense, weird situation. The young couple in my dream could very well have been the couple who died in the car crash, and my aunt's weakened, depressed state may have signalled her vulnerability to them. Could this deceased young couple have wanted my aunt to join them on the other side? I do ask myself what made it possible for me to enter this dream dimension to intervene and protect my aunt, and I have come to the belief that we can travel into other dimensions in our dream states to fulfill our spiritual tasks.

I had one final question for Aunt E, which was whether she was right- or left-handed. She was left-handed, which fit with my dream where she held the knife to her right wrist. I take this as further validation that this experience wasn't just a dream.

A Rumble in My Bedroom

Another time, I was asleep in my bed when I heard a female voice calling for help from inside my head. I awoke and tuned in to this call for help, aware that I was about to experience another waking dream. Sleep once again washed over me, and I saw a woman being attacked by a powerful, evil force emitting a massive amount of negative energy.

I heard voices (which I assumed were my spirit guides) warning me to stay clear of this evil force because it was "too strong, too powerful!" However, I have been informed by my personal spirit guides that my role when travelling into these other realms is to be a protector and Peaceful Warrior of God, so I willingly stayed in this dream state to protect this helpless woman.

I was fighting way above my weight class, but I mustered the courage to keep battling and moving forward toward this immense force. The closer I got, the more I felt the entity's tremendous destructive power. I managed to shove the woman out of harm's way, but now I was standing directly in front of my awesome opponent. I could feel the pain of my flesh beginning to tear away from my bones. It was too strong! I was in trouble, so I dug deep inside to find strength and courage.

I began to feel a stirring coming from my heart area, which turned into a protective vibration that emitted a low rumbling sound. Both the vibration and the sound continued to grow until I was able to meet this terrible, intimidating force head on. Then, with the vibrations still growing and the rumbling sound echoing through my chest, I awakened, safe in bed.

My wife woke up, instantly aware of the low, rumbling sound reverberating off the bedroom walls. She told me that the sound and vibration was not coming from my mouth, but rather seemed to emanate from my chest area.

It's important for me to remain skeptical of all these strange occurrences and to seek out validation wherever possible. Since my wife was a third-party witness to this event, I feel that this particular experience was validated.

I do wonder what caused the vibrating and the low rumbling sound which echoed off our bedroom walls, but thus far I have not found any answers. Perhaps more will be revealed to me in time.

Automatic drawing by author.

26

DAVE WONG

On December 12, 2006, I had a waking dream—a visitation. I was seated in a large auditorium, attending some kind of psychic convention or workshop, with my wife Val seated next to me. There was also quite a crowd around us. I didn't see anyone else I knew, but I did sense a group of people who felt very familiar. There was a centre court like you would find on a basketball court, and our seats looked down upon it.

My attention was drawn to the right. There was a gap, a space without chairs, and on the other side of it I saw my cousin Dee in one of the seats. She was looking at me and talking, trying to tell me something, but I couldn't hear as she was sitting too far away. I leaned slightly toward her to listen, and at this point I was telepathically made aware that I should *remember*.

It then became dark, as if the auditorium lights were turned down, and my seat reclined so that I was facing the ceiling. The spirit of my dad appeared to me, bringing with him an older Chinese man whom I didn't recognize, though I had the distinct feeling they were close. I wondered in my dream state if he was one of Dad's brothers, even though he didn't look like any of them. Then the name Dave came through, and I was once again telepathically made aware that I should *remember*.

During experiences like this, even though I'm in a dream-like state, I'm also aware of being half-awake in my bedroom. At this time, I had the familiar sensation that someone was in our bedroom.

I opened my eyes and there, standing at the foot of our bed, was a young Asian male wearing a plaid shirt with trousers. I could only make out the right side of his face. I blurted out a startled sound, which surprised the entity and caused him to disappear. I then made myself wake up completely and looked around the room. Feeling disappointed in myself for being startled during this visitation, I returned immediately to the dream-like state, hoping to reconnect with my visitors.

I found myself back at the auditorium, but this time on the top floor which was made of wood. The small, familiar-looking group went around a corner, beckoning me to follow them. As I neared the corner, the walls disappeared, and I suddenly found myself looking over the edge of a deep chasm. I have a fear of heights, so this frightened me. The group called me to follow them around to the other side, but the walls were gone so I would have to scale the railings to get around. An open hand appeared and offered to help me; I agreed to go to the other side, but I didn't take the hand. Instead, I was determined to get around by myself. As I made my way around, the hand remained near me, offering reassurance and seeming to guide me. And as I let go of the railing and stood on the floor, I could hear applause from the group.

When Val and I awoke in the morning, I told her about my dream. I wondered if perhaps my uncle Dave (one of Dad's brothers) had died, but I was confused because he didn't look like my uncle Dave. This was a *young* man who stood at my bed, accompanied by my dad and this other older man. I planned to phone around later that day to find out if anything had happened to Uncle Dave, but I was babysitting my grandson that morning, so I had to put those plans off.

Then, around 10 a.m., the phone rang. It was my cousin Dee, asking if I had heard the sad news. She was looking through the newspaper and noticed that our cousins were mentioned—one of their sons had died. His name was Dave Wong.

So, that's why I was to remember the name Dave. I thought it was my uncle Dave who had passed away, but it was really my cousin's son. I also realized that the reason I had seen Dee trying to tell me something from a distance is that she was the one who would phone me (from a distance) to tell me the news.

Another possible explanation came while talking with Dee the following day. I found out that Dave had been killed during a head-on collision with another car while he was driving home from work. Perhaps the reason I could only see half his face was because it was somehow damaged from this collision.

Finally, I'm pretty sure that the older Chinese man who had a connection to my dad wasn't any of Dad's brothers; he was probably either one of Dave's grandfathers or a great-grandfather. Whoever he was, I believe he and Dad brought Dave to me to communicate that he is now in a safe environment. I regret being so startled, causing us to lose connection. I did reconnect with Dave's spirit to apologize, but perhaps it is enough to know Dave is safely on the other side with his loved ones.

There are times when questions arise in Warrior's mind.
OK to question – but NEVER DOUBT!

27

MESSAGE IN A DREAM

In 1970, my beloved grandmother (Poa Poa) was in the hospital dying of cancer. I wanted her to know how much I loved her, so I did a watercolour painting of a bouquet of flowers and brought it to her. She smiled sweetly at me and told me she really liked it. Sadly, Poa Poa passed away the following day.

This was the first time I had painted with watercolours, and since it was special to me, I decided it would be the last time.

After Poa Poa passed away, my Aunt A phoned to tell me that something weird had happened while she was driving home with a box of Poa Poa's belongings, including the painting and a vase of flowers. Someone had cut in front of her car, forcing her to swerve and slam on the brakes to avoid an accident. This caused the vase to tip over, spilling the water out. She pulled her car over to assess the damage and was shocked to see that the water had splashed only on my painting, leaving all the other contents in the box untouched and dry. In addition, the image I painted of the bouquet of flowers had disappeared, leaving the canvas completely blank!

I told her it was impossible not only for the water to wash away the complete painting but also for it to leave everything else untouched. This was too far-fetched!

How could a splash of water dissolve all the paint? Why were none of her other belongings affected?

I drove to my Aunt A's apartment to check this out for myself, and sure enough, everything was exactly as she described. My aunt suggested that Poa Poa had taken the painting with her to Heaven; I found that hard to believe, but even harder to dismiss. Some things cannot be rationalized or satisfactorily explained. We can only accept them as they are and keep our minds open to the possibilities.

This event was instrumental to my spiritual growth because it expanded my realm of possibilities, and I became aware that not all truths can be scientifically proven (at least not at the present time).

Shared Dream

The passing of my Poa Poa was devastating to me. I grieved deeply for her, wondering if she was okay on the other side. Then, shortly after her passing, I had a memorable dream.

In this dream, I heard my name being called and found myself floating down a long, narrow hallway, just inches from the ceiling. I was being drawn toward a tiny, closed door, and as I approach, the door opens to show a small room fitted with a tiny bed. My Aunt E was lying face up on the bed with her eyes closed and her lips slightly apart. I hear the familiar voice of my Poa Poa coming out of my Aunt E's unmoving lips, saying, *"Don't worry, she's okay, everything's all right."* Then, I awoke. I laid awake for the rest of the night, wondering if this was a dream or if it was real.

The next morning, I phoned my Aunt E and arranged to have lunch with her so that I could tell her all about my dream. As soon as we sat down for lunch, Aunt E asked me to tell her about it. I related to her how my name was called, then I was drawn down a long hallway to a small door which opened as I approached. At that point she interrupts me by saying, ". . . and I'm lying on a bed, and your Poa Poa's voice is coming through me, telling you not to worry, that she's okay."

I was shocked! I gasped, "How do you know what I dreamt?"

She said calmly, "Because, I had the same dream last night. Your Poa Poa gave you this message so that you won't worry about her so much,"

I don't know what (or who) allowed Poa Poa to send us this message in a dream. Could this indicate that we are all connected, even after death, and that it is possible to communicate with loved ones on the other side? Since my aunt and I both had the same dream on the same night, I'm confident that I was truly in contact with Poa Poa.

We are able to receive messages from our loved ones in many ways—dreams are only one method. They come to us from the other side to offer love and protection, and to receive it, we need only to remain open to making a connection.

Automatic drawing by author.

Protected by Her Spirit

At this time in my life, I was living in an apartment building that always gave me the heebie-jeebies. I dreaded having to walk through the hallways as I would sense hands and faces coming out of the walls. Whenever I was riding alone in the elevator, I would have the feeling I wasn't *really* alone. The underground parking and storage areas were the scariest places to be as I would feel entities gather around me, grabbing at me for attention. Friends and family would laugh at me whenever I mentioned this, saying that I had too much imagination. They thought I was just spooked out because a funeral home happened to be located at the opposite end of the block.

As it turns out, there's good reason why this apartment building gave me the willies. I found out some time later that the land my apartment building was situated on had previously been part of the funeral home, and the parking area was used to store the dead bodies. So much for "too much imagination"!

A few days after Poa Poa passed away, I came home to my apartment after work. As I walked into the kitchen, I sensed something floating in the air. It appeared as a clear bubble, like a balloon with the skin removed—a smaller version of what I would later encounter at the mountain—and I instantly recognized it as the essence of Poa Poa. She telepathically prompted me to leave the apartment and head to the dreaded underground parking area. Poa Poa's presence gave me a sense of being protected, so this time I felt absolutely no fear as I calmly walked down the hallway and rode the elevator to the underground parking.

As I stepped into the parking area, she told me to walk between all the parked cars, which I did. I felt no fear at all during my rounds as I somehow realized that I was protected from harm. She then communicated telepathically, *"No fear. I am here with you always. I am watching over you and protecting you."*

This experience further strengthened my belief that there is contact available with loved ones on the other side, and they connect with us to lend strength and confidence to help us walk this earthly plane with strong strides.

28

CONTACT WHILE IN A COMA

My Aunt A was afflicted with Alzheimer's for many years, and toward the end of her life she was living in a care home. In June 2011, she lost the ability to drink or swallow food on her own, which meant it was just a matter of time before she would cross over.

On June 26, family members gathered around her bedside. She was in and out of a coma, so she wasn't able to talk. Some of my family members are skeptical of the concept that we can communicate with each other through telepathy, so I decided against communicating with her in front of everyone else to avoid any possible awkwardness.

When everyone left, though, I stayed behind and connected with her, asking if she had a message for the family. She responded, *"Each individual family member is like a flower. The petals of the flower represent each individual's unique personality traits, experiences, and talents. When all the individual flowers gather together in love, we create a family bouquet—and what a wonderful bouquet it is!"*

On July 1, my wife Val and I stopped by the care home on the way to a family BBQ. We asked the nurses how my aunt was doing, and they all said that based on their experience, she wasn't ready to cross over yet. I then connected with Aunt A, who communicated that she would leave this earthly plane "before the next day," so I approached the nurses with this message. They were all adamant that she wasn't ready to die yet, but I trusted Aunt A's message. So, I telepathically told my aunt that I planned to come back that evening to sit with her so that she wouldn't have to leave this world alone.

Arriving back home, I felt drained of energy. I glanced at the clock, and it was only 4 p.m., so I decided to take a short nap and then drive back to see my aunt after dinner. Quickly falling asleep on the couch, I entered into a waking dream state. The couch began spinning in slow circles, and two spirits came forward. They felt loving and had a familiar energy to them, so I had no fear. The two spirits came closer, and I knew I should go with them.

Suddenly I awoke. I thought that I had napped for maybe half an hour, but to my surprise, the clock revealed it was 10:30 p.m.! I shot up off the couch, worried that it was too late to drive in to visit my aunt. Then, the phone rang. It was my uncle, Aunt A's brother, calling to tell me that my aunt had just passed away.

Perhaps my aunt had a hand in me falling asleep for such a long time. Maybe she sheltered me from the discomfort of sitting with her all evening at her bedside. Or perhaps she was protecting me from the grief I would feel at the moment of her death, but somehow allowed me to witness her last moment before being accompanied to the other side.

I took this experience as a reminder to trust in the truth of our communication rather than automatically taking the word of others. The words "no doubt," which I received on the mountain after finding Bachan, came to mind. I believe that it's possible for humans in comas to communicate telepathically, and that this is an area requiring further research.

Pondering my aunt's words describing our family being like flowers, I drew a parallel between my family and humankind in general. Each of us has a "tone," and try as we might to all be the same, no two of us are exactly alike. But it is better for us to be unique anyway—if we were all the same, the world would become monotonous. Instead, if we all work together and act out of love, our individual notes can combine into a beautiful harmony.

Automatic drawing by author.

This wasn't the end of my communications with Aunt A. We held a dinner to celebrate Aunt A's life at her favourite Chinese restaurant. During the dinner, my cell phone rang, and I saw my aunt's name on the display. I thought it was just a coincidence—I must have unintentionally pocket-dialled her number.

When dinner came to a close, my phone emitted an unfamiliar chiming sound. Upon checking my phone, the display showed a calendar reminder for my aunt's dinner. However, I never entered that reminder because I didn't know how to use that function! My assumption is that Aunt A was keeping in contact from the other side, letting me know that she was aware of and acknowledging her Celebration of Life.

29

WARNING FROM THE OTHER SIDE

At various times, I'll notice a slight sound or smell in the room which triggers my spiritual antennae. When nobody else in the room notices any of these sensations, I become aware that a spirit might be trying to come through or get my attention.

One evening, as I was watching TV, I noticed the smell of cigarettes burning. I asked Val if she smelled anything; when she said no, my antennae went up. I noticed the cigarette smell again the following evening, and once again, Val couldn't smell anything unusual. I wondered who was trying to contact me. I don't have a habit of actively seeking out spirits, but I do try to figure out who's trying to come through, then open my energy field to them.

The following day, I felt a sudden urge for some won ton soup, so I drove to one of my favourite Chinese restaurants in Langley. When the waiter came to my table to take my order, I told him I was craving a bowl of won ton. We went over the various won ton bowls on the menu, and I chose the large bowl of seafood won ton. As he walked away, he called out, "Okay, one large bowl of seafood won ton for you!"

I involuntarily called out, "No, I mean a large bowl of fish maw soup!"

The waiter stopped, confused. "I thought you wanted seafood won ton soup, not fish maw soup." I apologized and replied that I changed my mind, so off he went to get me fish maw soup.

As I sat at the table, confused by my sudden change of menu choice, it suddenly dawned on me: Maw! Of course! My friend Jason and his mother had had a very close relationship. He called her Maw, which became a nickname that stuck—all of Jason's friends and relatives called her Maw as well. She was also a chain smoker, which accounted for the smell of cigarette smoke. I realized that Maw's spirit must be attempting to contact me because Jason was dealing with heart issues, going in and out of the hospital as he looked for answers. I drove home, made contact with her spirit, and told her I was open to communication from her.

That night, while lying in my bed with my body and mind open and receptive, Maw's spirit came forward. She frantically told me that the doctors must be informed that they're missing the exact location of Jason's problem. She then pointed to the area a few inches to the right of my heart and said this was the spot they needed to look at.

The following day, I called Jason and related Maw's important message to him. He said that he couldn't expect the specialists to believe this, so he never passed the message on. Weeks later, while walking down the hallway, Jason collapsed and died of heartrelated issues. No autopsy was performed, but I can only assume that Maw had pointed to the correct spot.

The bonds of love continue in the afterlife, and Jason and his mother had an unusually strong bond. It stands to reason that she would be in his surrounds, protecting him from harm.

Presence

It's quite common for people to notice the presence of loved ones who've crossed over. It may also be through smells, such as perfumes, cigars, or cigarettes. It may be feelings of being touched or the sounds of familiar voices. A client of mine whose beloved dog had recently passed on claimed that he sometimes heard his dog barking when he entered the house. Some people may feel that their deceased loved ones are contacting them by leaving objects such as coins laying around or by facilitating sight-

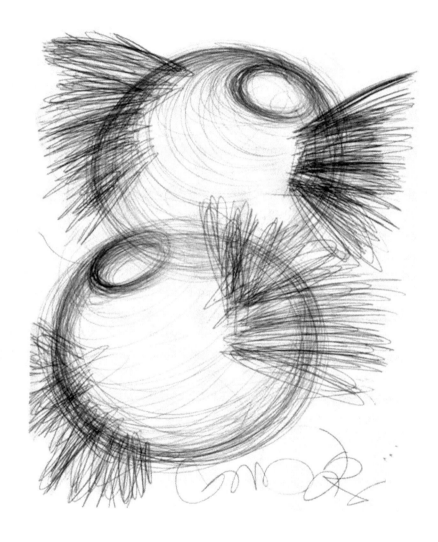

Automatic drawing by author.

ings of butterflies, dragonflies, or birds. Others have noticed lights flickering on and off or had their TV affected. I believe that these experiences are not just wishful thinking or figments of their imagination, but rather actual connections with their deceased loved ones.

After the passing of my sister Judy and my niece Bailey, I closed my Karate club for a week. On the day classes were to commence again, I was concerned that my sadness and grief would affect my students negatively, so I sat at the foot of my bed to meditate lightly and restore my inner strength.

I went into an altered state and found myself on what appeared to be a mountain top that was a meeting spot for the spirits of those who had just crossed over and their loved ones. My sister Judy appeared facing me. We both began floating sideways in a standing position facing each other, travelling through beautiful, flowing rivers of colour the likes of which I had never seen before. All the while, Judy was telepathically sending me information. Suddenly, we came to an abrupt stop. Judy told me that she was to continue on, and that I wasn't allowed to follow. Wanting to be with her, my arms instantly reached out to grab her, but I instead found myself being thrown backwards onto my bed and my spirit being shot back into my chest. For some reason I can't recall everything Judy told me, but I definitely felt her love. She's visited me a few times since and is responsible for producing the automatic drawing which has become the front cover of this book.

My niece Bailey has also visited me, usually through dreams but also through my automatic writings. She also signed her name on the drawing on the front cover.

Write talk act do think
all these are yours to do!!
Go out --- display wings
--- Straighten out wings and
fly homeward !!!!!

Automatic drawing by author.

CONCLUSION

I have covered many topics in this book, which might be overwhelming and confusing to some. So, I will summarize the most important points to create an easy reference.

In Part 1, I shared that many of us feel helpless, hopeless, and powerless to take any action toward achieving peace in our troubled world. I also shared one key piece of information which could unlock our unlimited human potential, give us the power to change this world, and to give us hope: the simple fact that we are ALL ONE! We are indeed different, but we are not separate. Each of us is a single flower contributing to the beautiful garden or an individual note in a harmonious melody. Once we realize that we are truly ALL ONE, and that we are not ALONE, hope enters and negative energy diminishes. In that moment, we learn that we have power.

I also discussed that in order to be a conscious creator in life, we need to become aware of energy. Everything we come across, both living and inanimate, is made of energy, and energy can be manipulated by our awareness and intention. We have the power to shift, change, clear, and release energy at any time. After all, we aren't just a body that *has* energy; we are conscious energy *being* human.

Each of us is a piece of the Divine Source—an individual wave in one ocean of energy. So, I presume that if we truly are a piece of the Divine Source, we must accept the fact that we also have been gifted with the power to become or accomplish whatever we envision. Along with this gift, we must accept the responsibility to use our power for peace and harmony in our world.

Also in Part 1, I shared that we each have the choice to live our Truth and become the highest version of ourselves. To achieve this, start by mindfully devoting yourself to the seeking of truth. Follow your heart instead of the herd and claim true knowledge over the cloak of ignorance.

Finally, I discussed a sacred space within each of us where our powerful Inner Warrior lies dormant. Our duty is to become aware of this Inner Warrior, and to honour and nurture it. We each have the potential to become a true Warrior for Peace—to call out for a harmonious, balanced world, and to leave a lasting legacy for future generations. The choice is ours to make.

In Part 2, I recalled my entry into the world of martial arts and shared some teachings that I gleaned from my studies. These ancient teachings still relate to our modern era and can be used to influence and strengthen our daily lives.

The key aspects of martial arts are also the key aspects of life. For example, in martial arts, I learned that technique alone is hollow without a solid foundation because you can then be easily uprooted and are limited by the memorization of techniques. Similarly, when our society focuses excessively on "techniques" (laws and rules of behaviour) to change our chaotic world, we neglect the actual root causes of our problems: our false beliefs. We must address our false beliefs about the separation—between ourselves and others, and between ourselves and the Divine Source—in order to change our world.

In martial arts, we also strive to create flexibility in our bodies. Similarly, in our society, we must strive for flexibility in our minds. Keeping an open mind—being open to the ideas and opinions of others—makes our daily lives more peaceful.

Also in this part, I recall my experience on the mountain where I encountered an entity appearing as a bubble. This entity shared valuable information with me regarding our relationship with others, and with the Divine Source.

I then shared with you the stories of Mary and Billy, who serve as examples of the power of using chi for healing. They are living proof that energy healing can be more effective if the subject is open to receiving healing energy and if there is no negative energy to overcome.

In Part 3, I discussed my role in providing energy healing sessions for people with health issues. During energy healing sessions, there is direct communication with Divine Source, which fosters inner calm and peace. While in this state, it is natural to do acts of love as we are in a state of unconditional love.

We are all capable of becoming energy healers. Achieving this comes down to mindfully feeling from our hearts, connecting with Source, and focusing our loving intentions on others.

I then shared that we can communicate with infants through telepathy. Infants and animals alike communicate through the medium of energy, and telepathy converts energy into language. As with animals, infants are sensitive to energy, so telepathic communication could become a useful tool in the future.

Also in Part 3, I related the story of my dry-land training sessions with a group of hockey players where I was reminded that wherever our attention goes (even unintentional attention), energy flows. We must be vigilant of our thoughts and intentions toward others as our emitted energy can adversely affect them if we are not careful.

In Part 4, I related stories of my telepathic communication with animals through the language of energy, which highlight their awareness, compassion, wisdom, and healing abilities. Our pets' prime concern is that their humans become aware that there is no holier moment than NOW! We must be mindful of the beauty of the moment.

I also shared that all species, including humans, are ALL ONE, and no species has more right to be here on Earth than any other. The same spark of life that is within us is within all our animal friends. The desire to live is the same within all of us.

The animal kingdom has requested that we tear down the invisible false walls which we have created. These false walls of ego and feelings of superiority separate humans from each other as well as from all other living beings, creating narrow, confining corridors which restrict the way we move through our human journeys. This is a very important message that we must seriously consider.

Many times, animals have gifted me with important life lessons through their wisdom and challenged me to stretch my mind. Energy is the universal language of all animals, so it's natural for them to receive and share energy healing without the negative energy of skepticism or apprehension. It is for these reasons I enjoy focusing on animal healing and communication.

I also shared that our pets protect us energetically. When we are sick, our pets defend us by pulling our sick energy from our bodies and bringing it into their energy field. Sometimes, when they can't quite manage to transform the sick energy into healthy energy, they wind up at the veterinary clinics to be euthanized.

In Part 5, I related some of my experiences which point to the possible existence of expressions of life and intelligent forces from beyond this earthly dimension. We live in a multi-dimensional universe, which Earth is but a small part of, so we should remind ourselves to keep an open mind.

Spirit beings from other worlds are in our surrounds, but most of us are unaware of their presence. We are all born with an innate psychic awareness, but for many, this awareness remains repressed. By opening to the invisible world of spirit, you will grow along your personal spiritual path.

We are able to communicate telepathically with those who are in a coma. I share, as an example, my Aunt A, who informed me when she was due to depart this earthly plane. I believe that many would benefit by researching this method of communication.

Finally, I believe that there is life beyond this physical world, and that our existence does not end with death. My experiences have shown me that our loved ones who've crossed over are at peace and wish only peace and joy for those of us still remaining here on Earth. And although they are no longer here with us, they are able to communicate with us through our dreams and energetic connections. We should never doubt that our loved ones are always staying near us, bringing protection and messages of love.

Automatic drawing by author.

Keep the message of hope
for the balance required to
make decisions judgements
for future of children and
to progress toward happiness
for all --- complete this
picture of reality so you will
notice the beauty in energy
and sky above & heaven
below --- nothing else to
be done but to protect
healing love energy ---
'''Force of love commands
many to action --- we are all
here together for purpose of
all new age of '''''.
Depend on it for strength
in future and let us
guide your fate in
endeavour to free all ---

Warriors for Peace

So, dear reader, I hope that my words have perhaps watered some of the Peaceful Warrior seeds that are already within you. Have confidence that you can make a difference in this world and come to be a laser beam shining out enlightenment and compassion for all beings. Dig deep within, panning the gold inside of yourself to harness your natural insight, passion, and wisdom in order to transform your life to benefit others.

To those of you who are seekers of the Truth, I hope you continue to practise and nurture the happiness and peace within you. Future generations will learn through the truth of our actions. We are the elders—the role models for the younger generations. We can *say* what we want, but it is our *actions* which reflect our true intentions.

As surely as the shadow accompanies the body, result accompanies action. What we've done in the past has created the present. What we choose to do now will affect our future.

Each human on Earth can choose their own path in life, and that's what makes us unique. Remember that your spirit is the truth, and by identifying with this truth, you will progress on your spiritual journey. I can only view and speak from my own spot on the mountain of life, and hopefully what I'm sharing will be of some benefit to us all. I realize that what I'm illustrating here is my way—my Do. It is not necessarily the best or only way; it's just another way.

I encourage you to find your own unique way. Begin to make decisions which are functional—that are in harmony with Love. Once you can decide what your purpose is in life, BELIEVE in your choice; have no doubt! In time, the need to grow and mature will make itself known. Remember that you are "walking a crooked smile," and that the obstacles you face will help you expand your knowledge and approach life in a new way. Every new day is a gift to us, so we should strive to learn through our personal experiences and live in a way that makes joy and happiness possible.

You are a spiritual being on a journey to enlightenment, so uncover the Peaceful Warrior within and express who you really are in an honest and creative way. This is the greatest gift you can offer the world—and yourself! In the end, I hope my words and illustrations have assisted you, even in some small way, on your personal journey toward peace and well-being.

Clues? No clues are necessary —
we already hold the answers within.

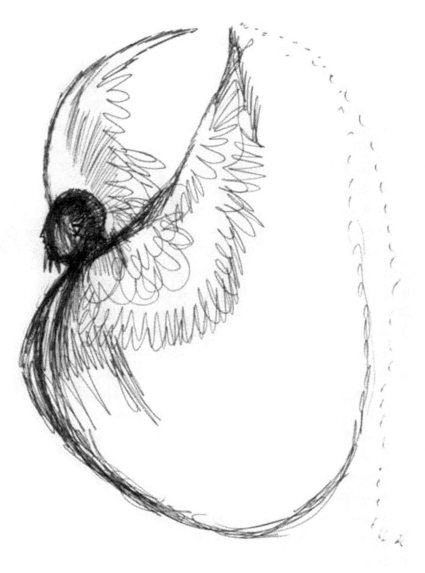

Automatic drawing by author.

Author and KT bowing to each other in the dojo.

ABOUT THE AUTHOR

For much of his life, Jerry Wong has been deeply involved in the areas of graphic arts and design, martial arts, intuitive energy healing, telepathic animal communication, and Chi Kung (the study of life force energy). These areas of study have influenced Jerry profoundly, and he is grateful for his experiences as they have benefitted him in many ways. He especially acknowledges the animal kingdom for placing their trust in his heart and for challenging his existing paradigms.

Jerry has attained valuable insights by opening to his inner navigation system and continues to walk his spiritual path while nurturing the Peaceful Warrior within.

CPSIA information can be obtained
at www.ICGtesting.com
Printed in the USA
BVHW012340170722
642384BV00010B/425

9 781778 154706